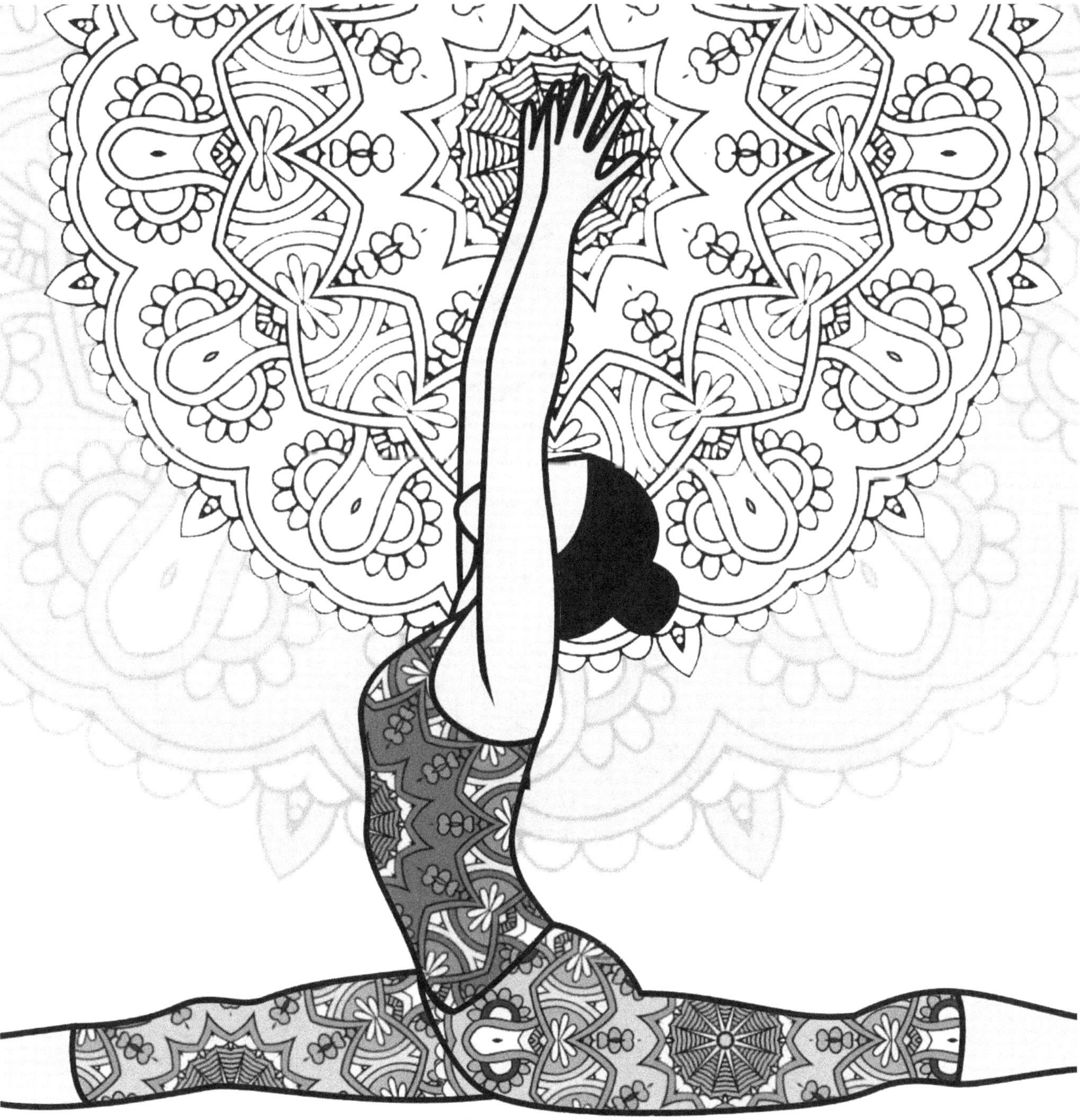

YOGA

FLORAL MANDALAS

COLORING BOOK FOR ADULTS

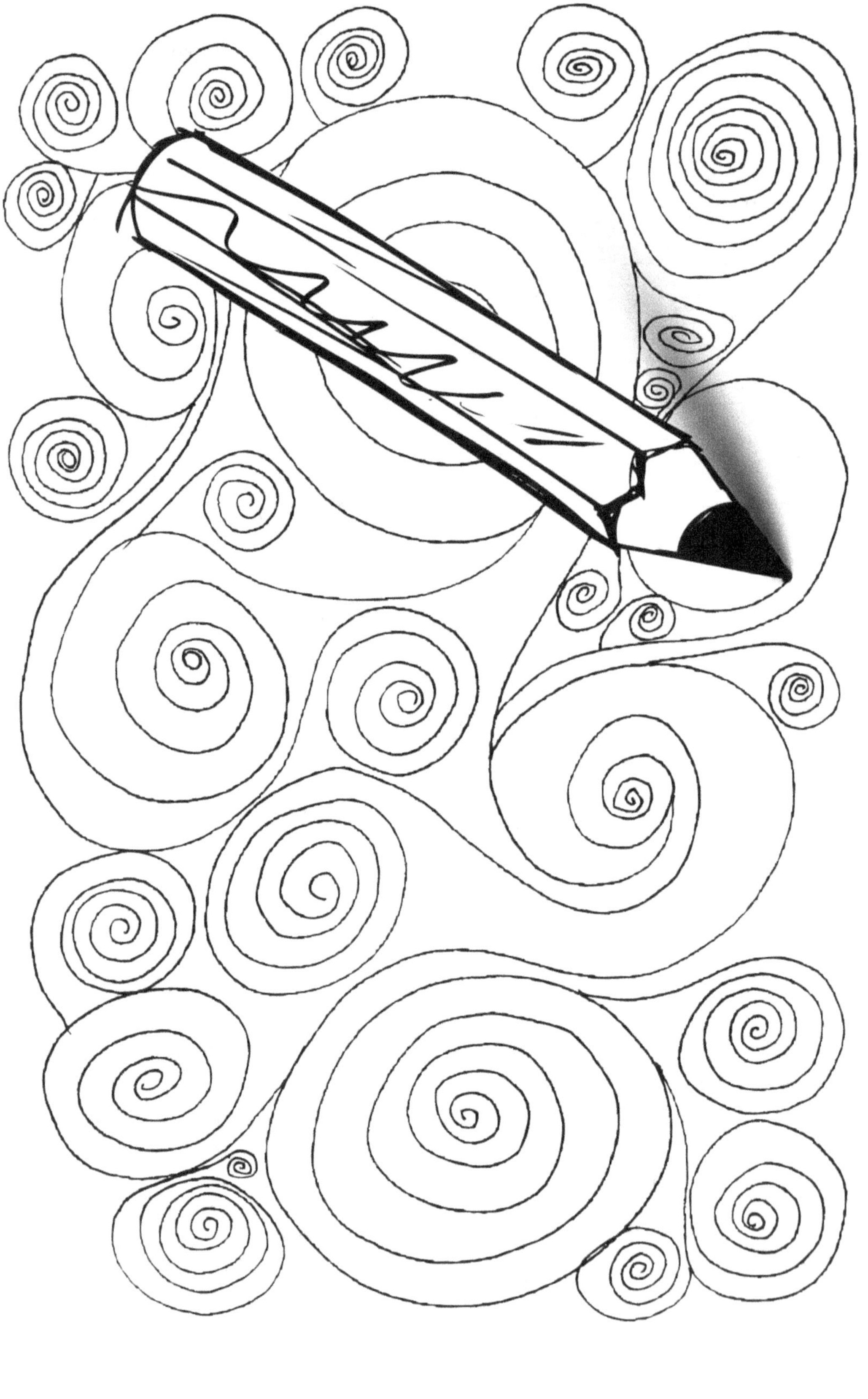

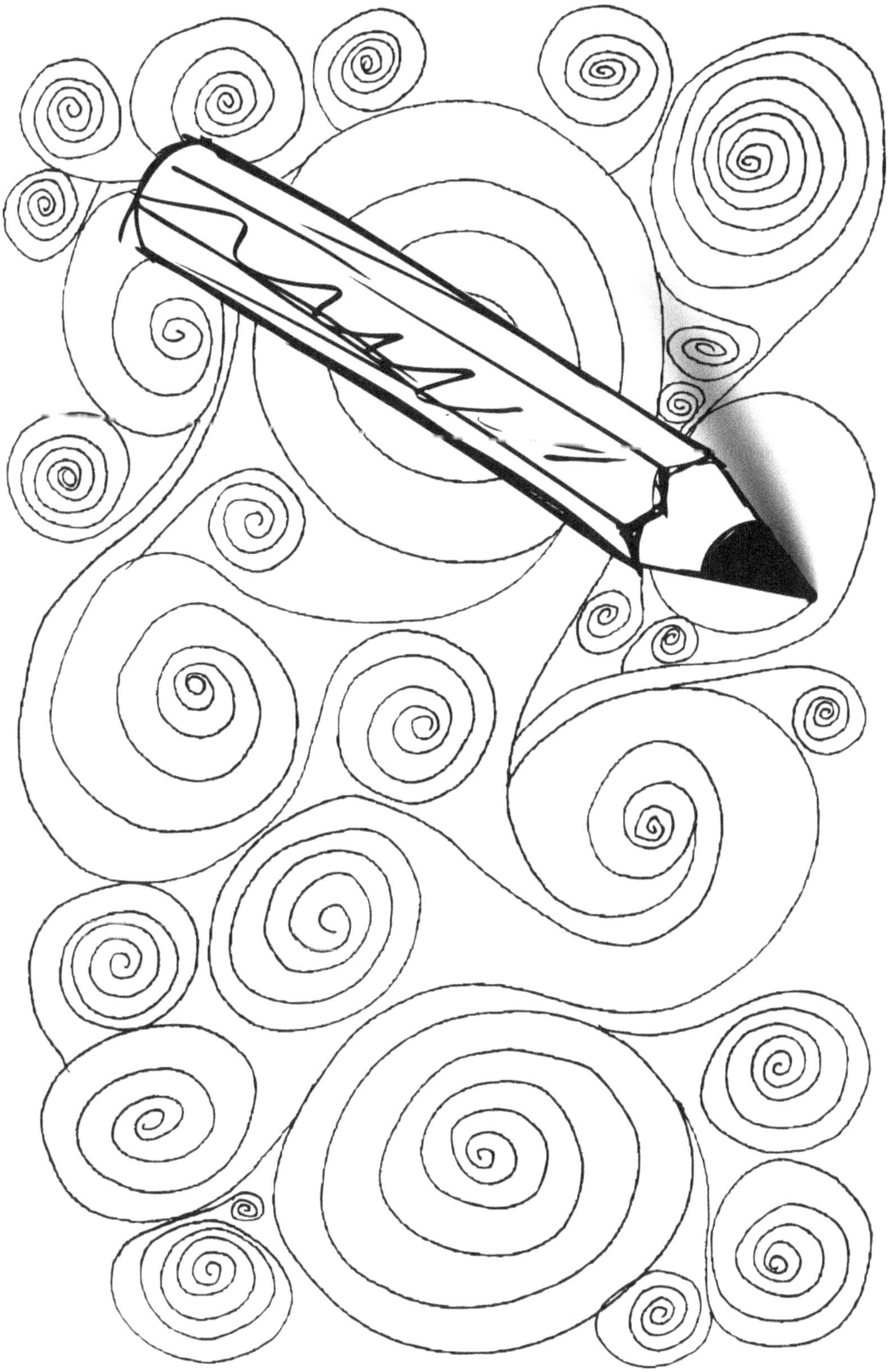

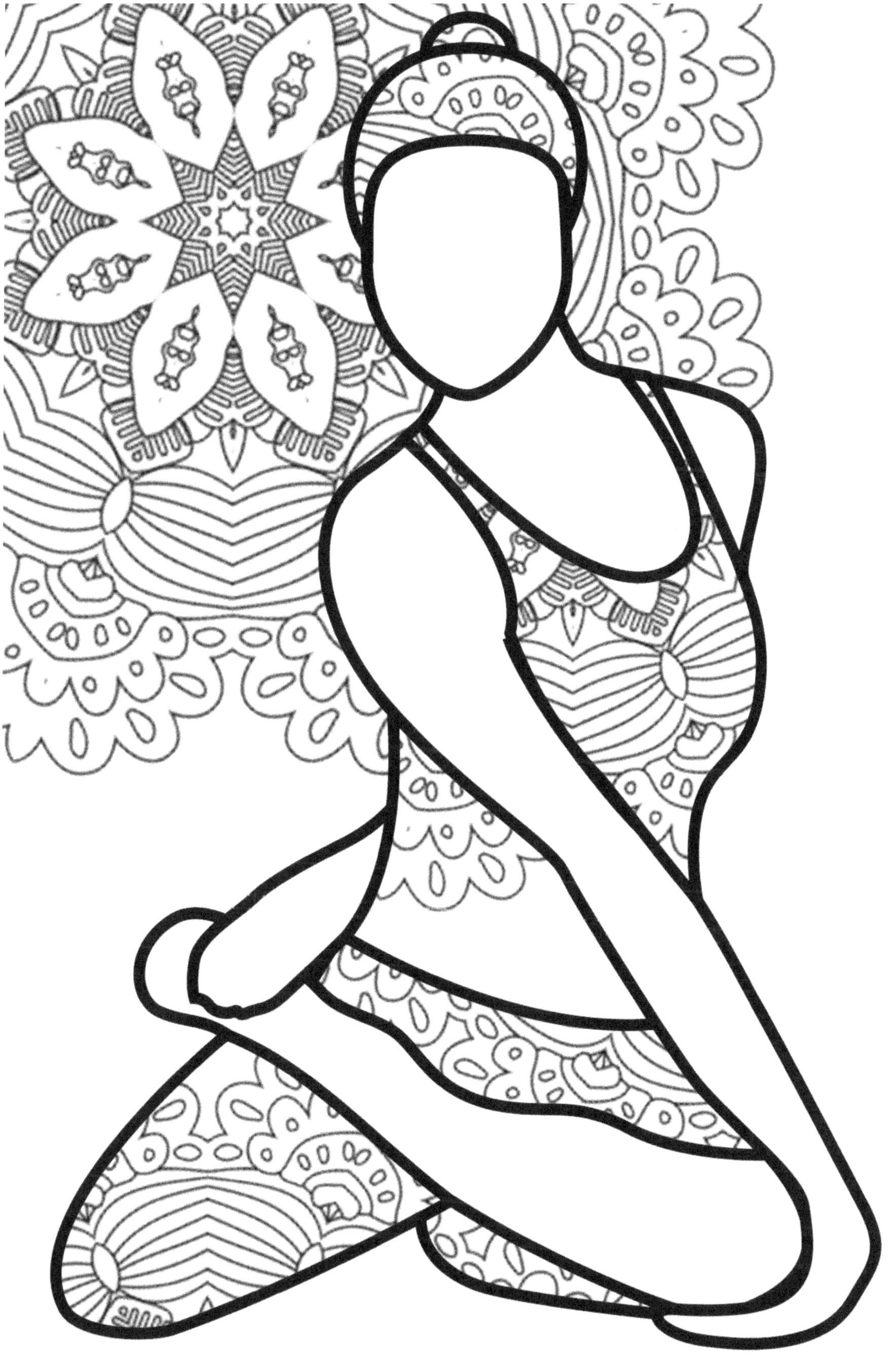

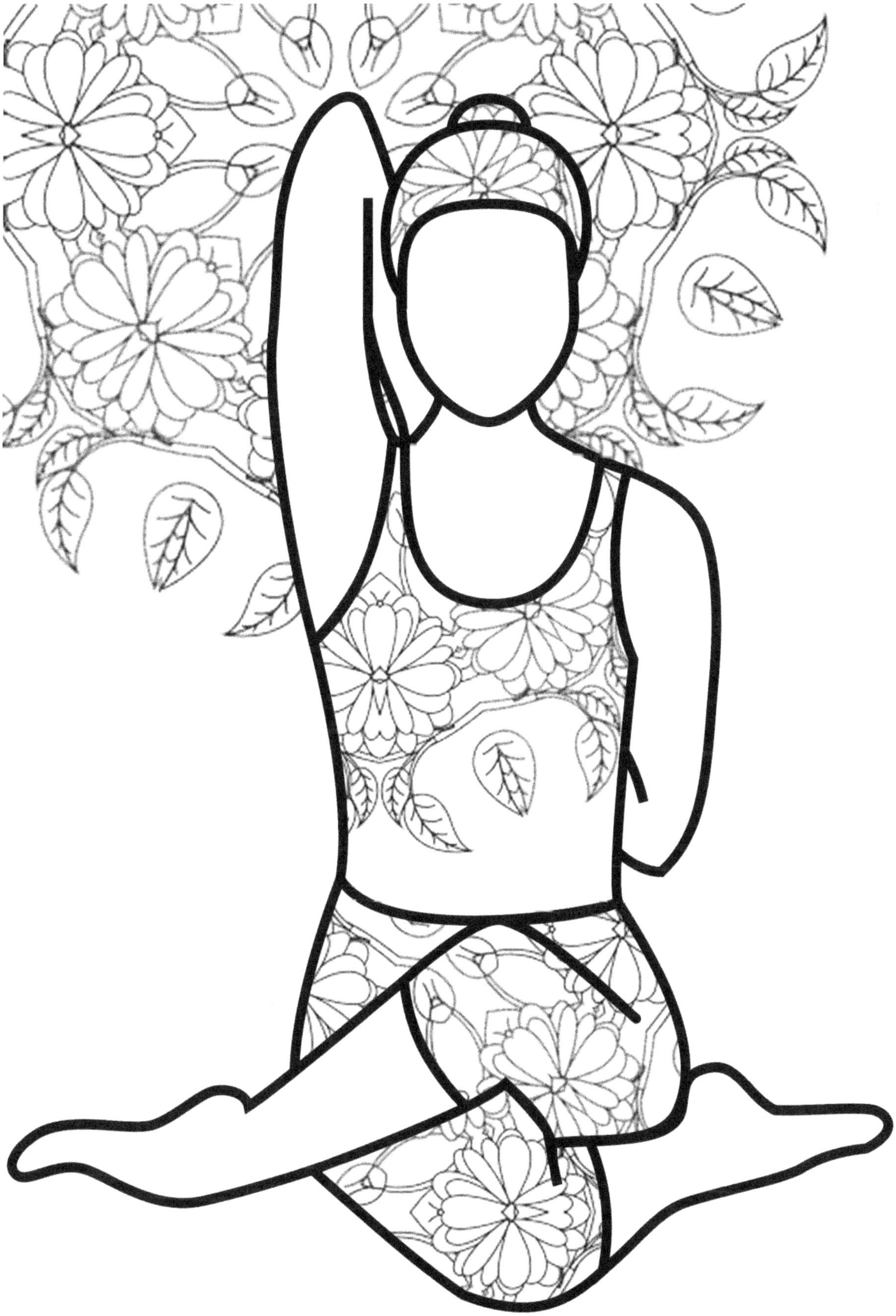

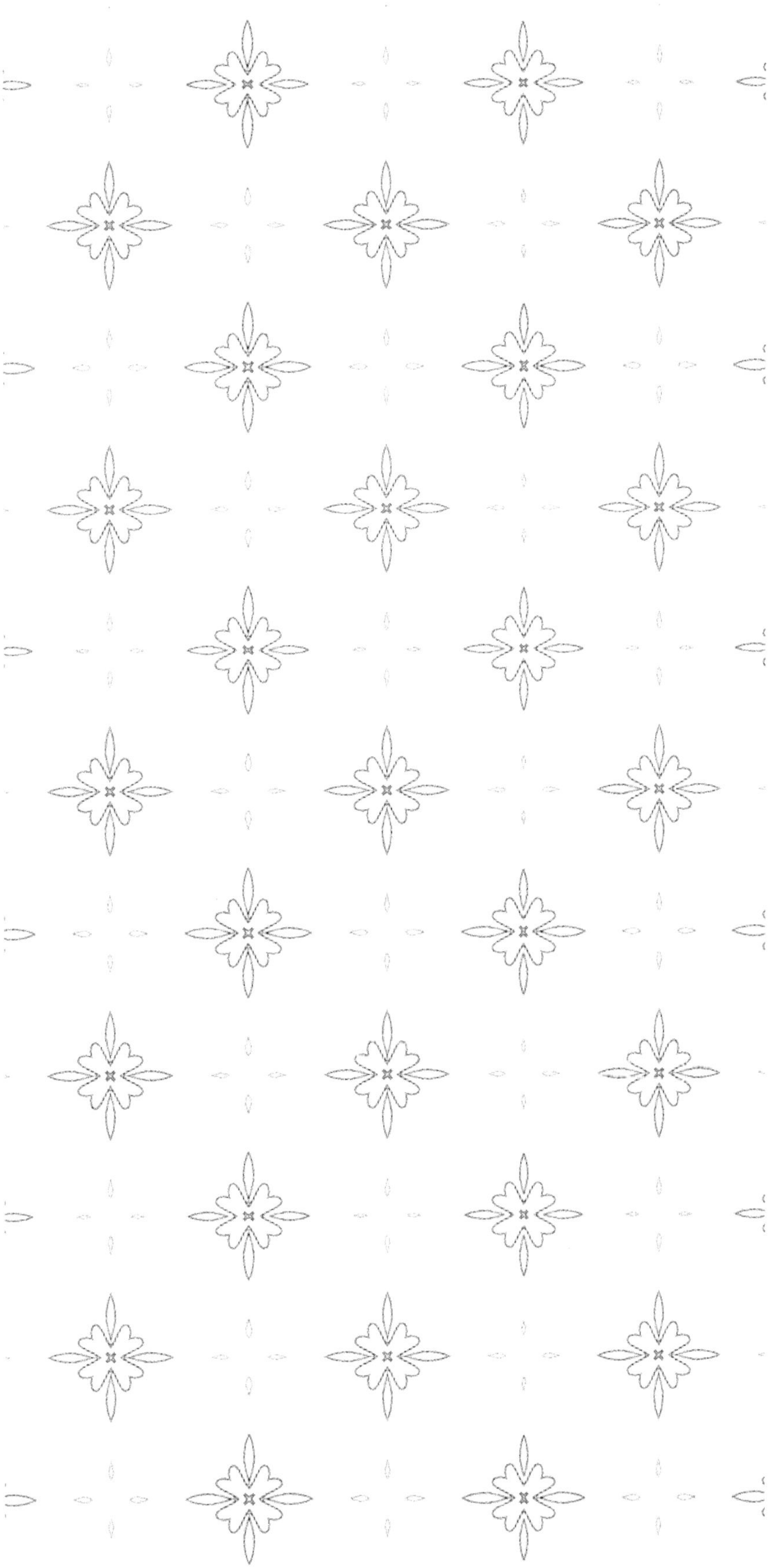

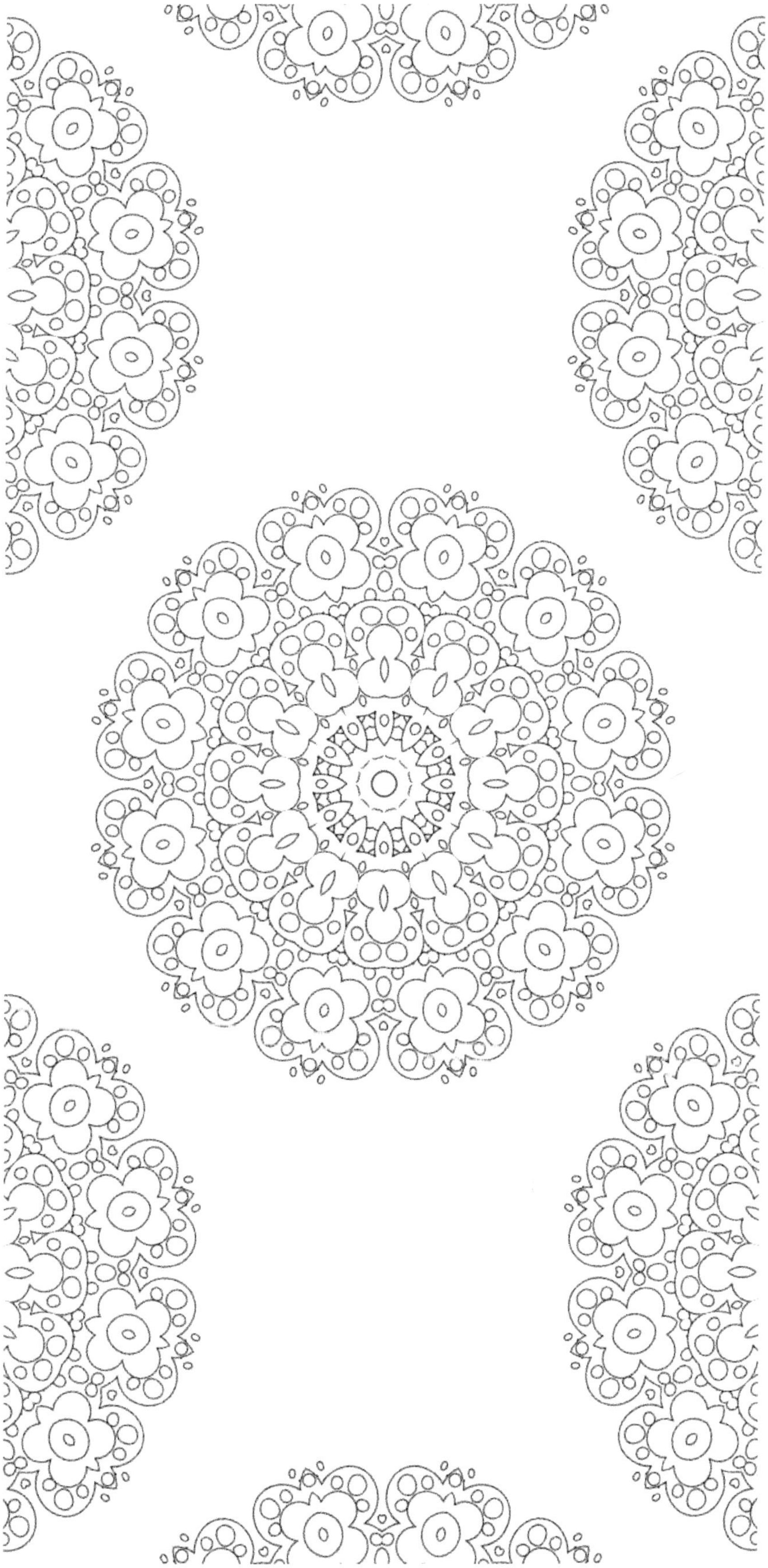

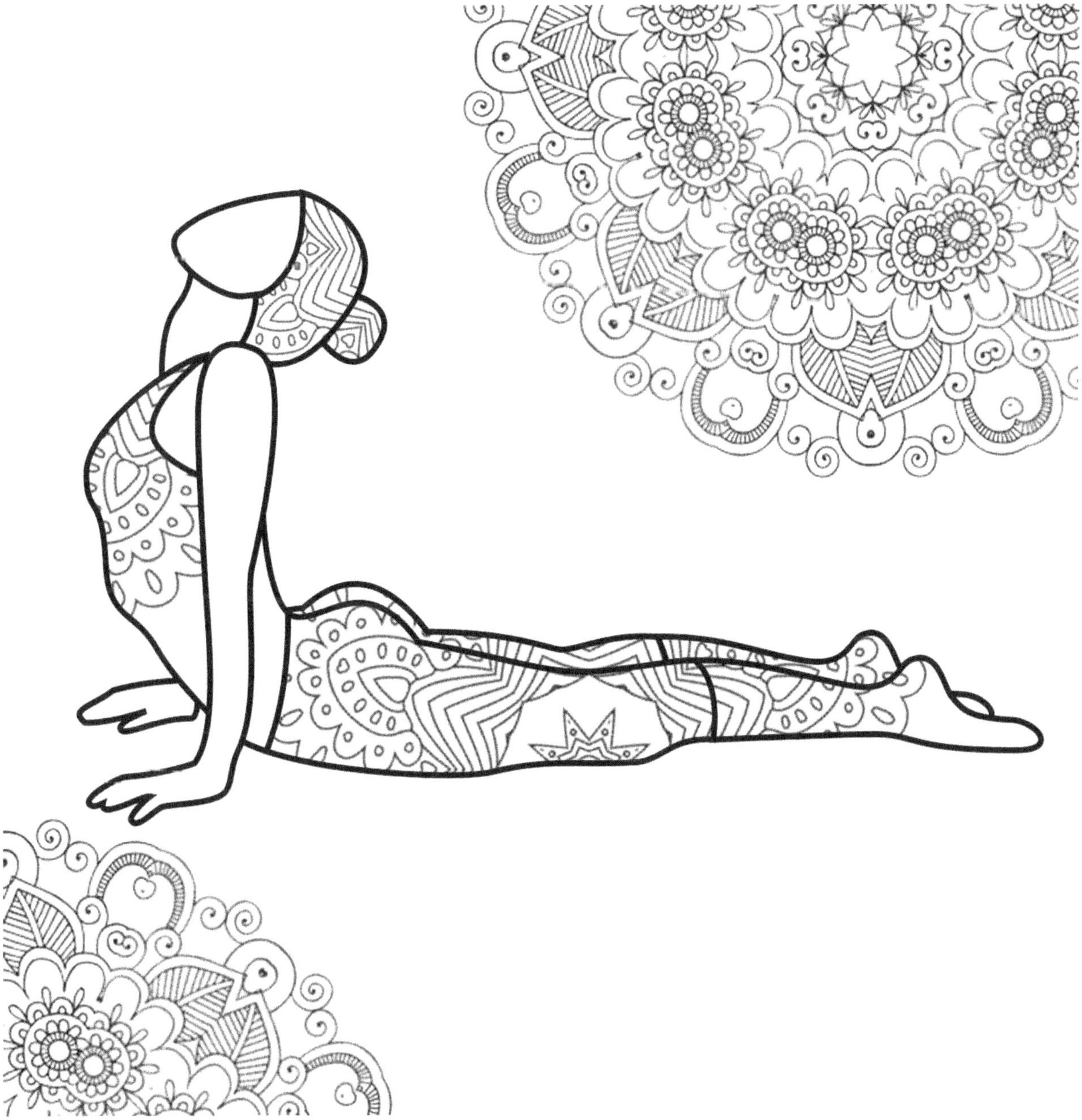

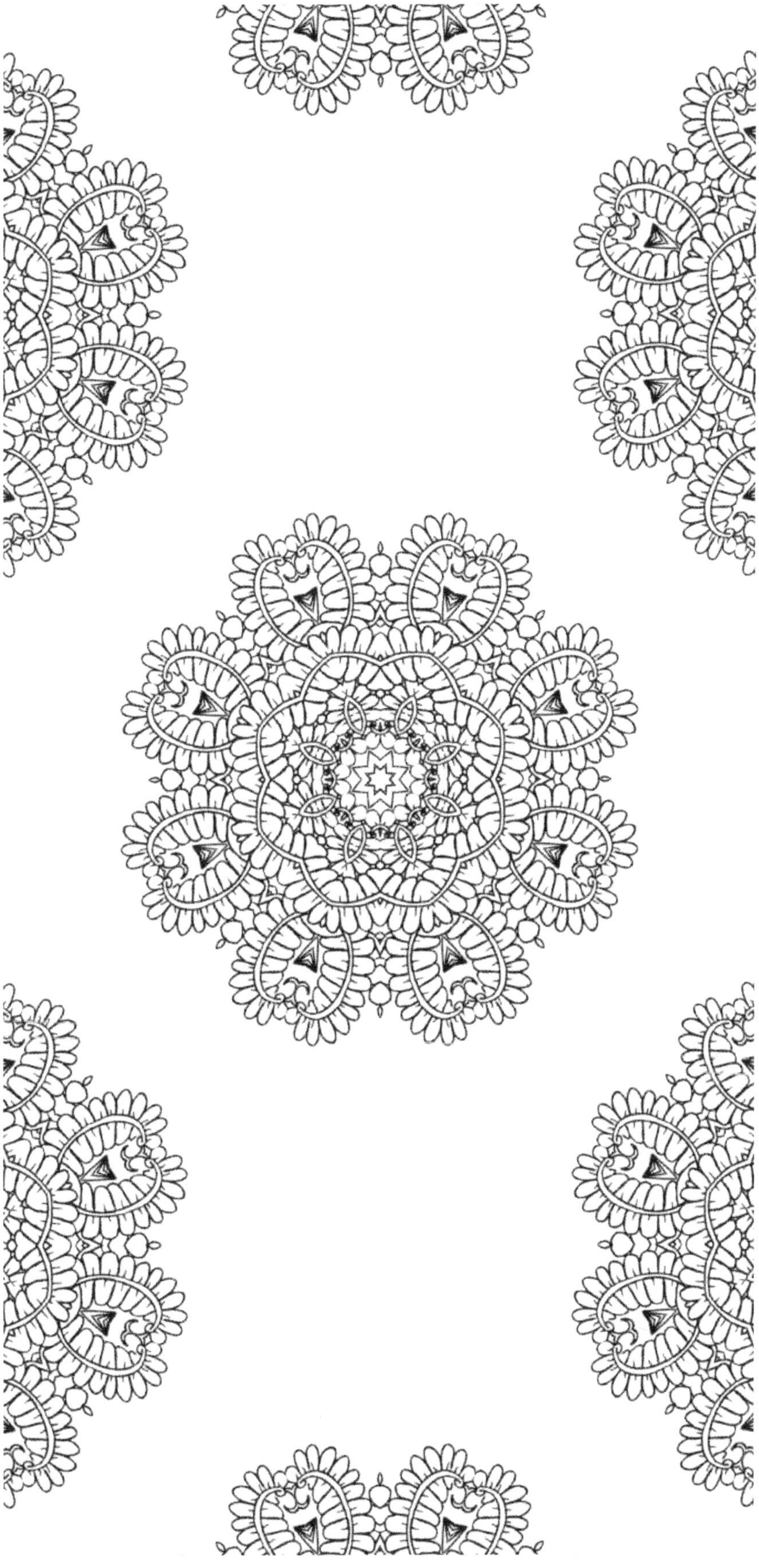

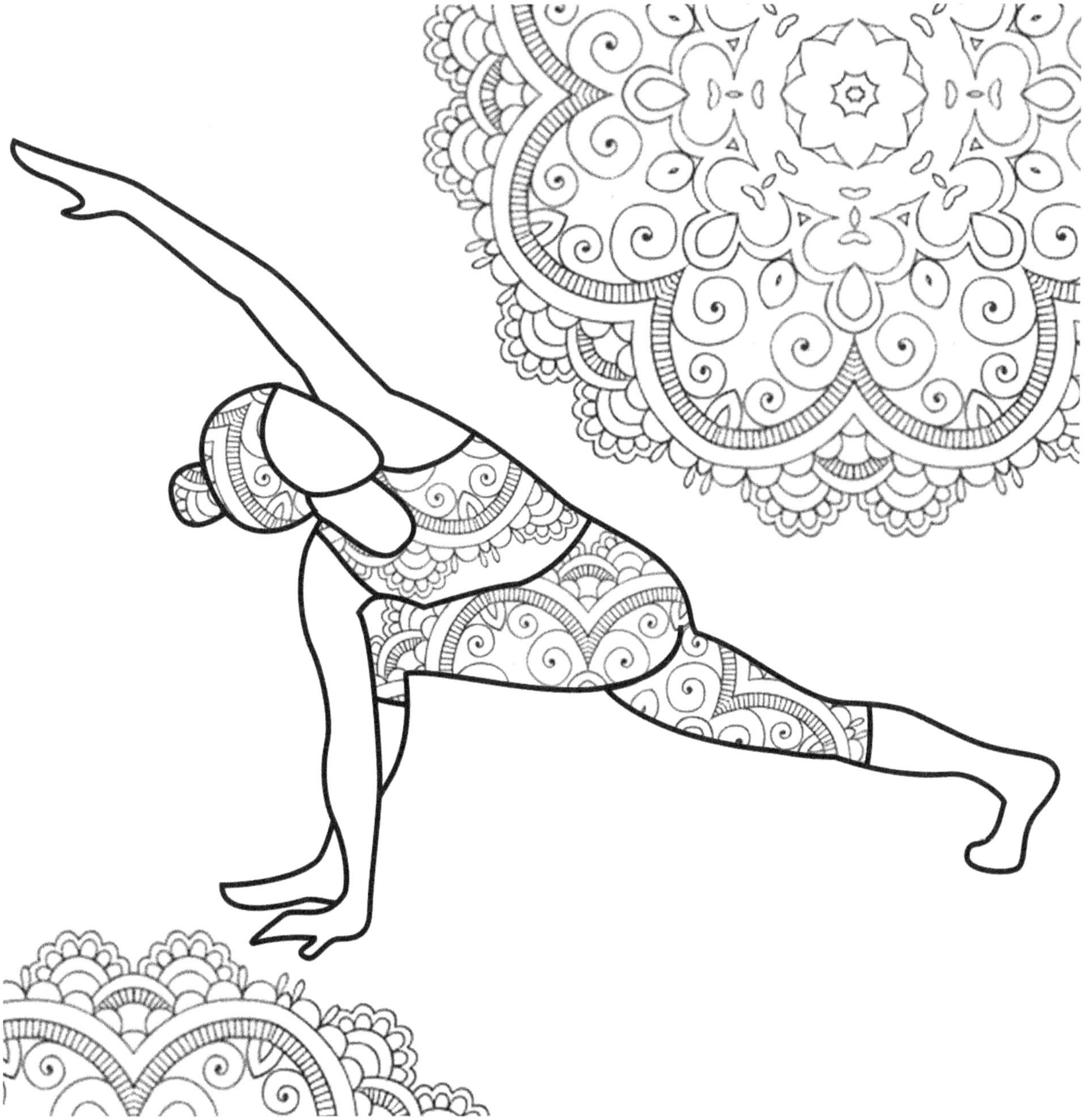

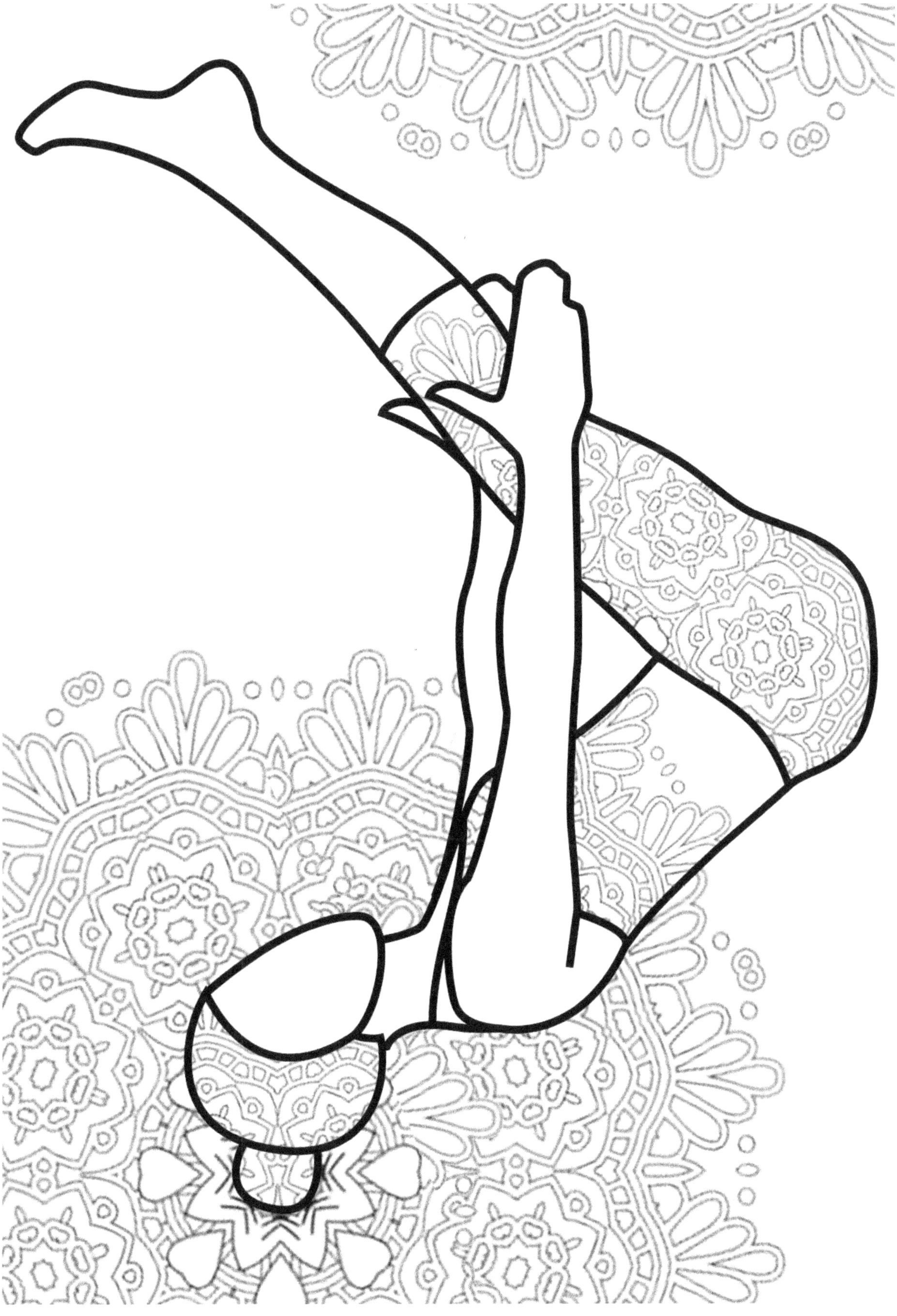

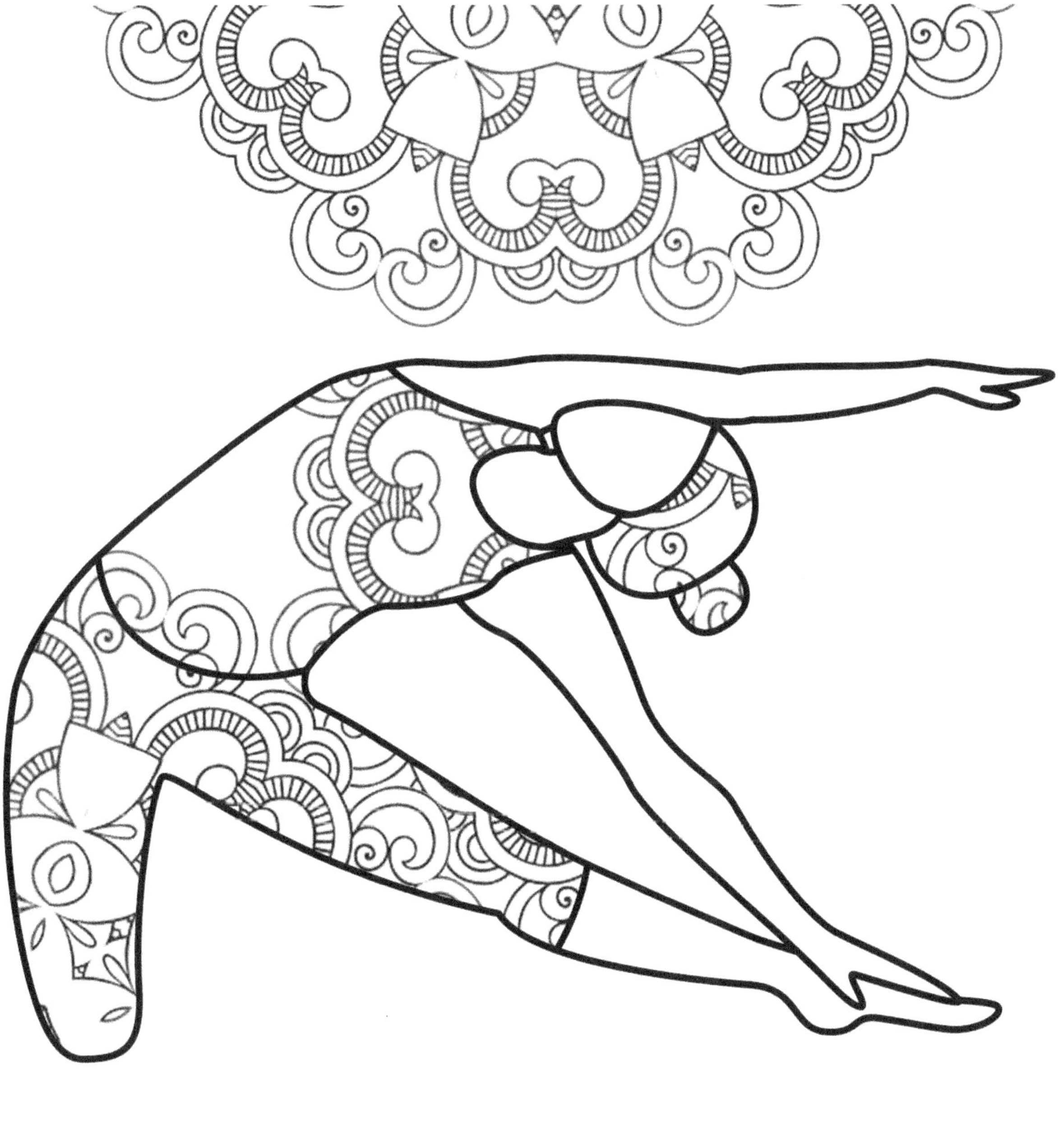

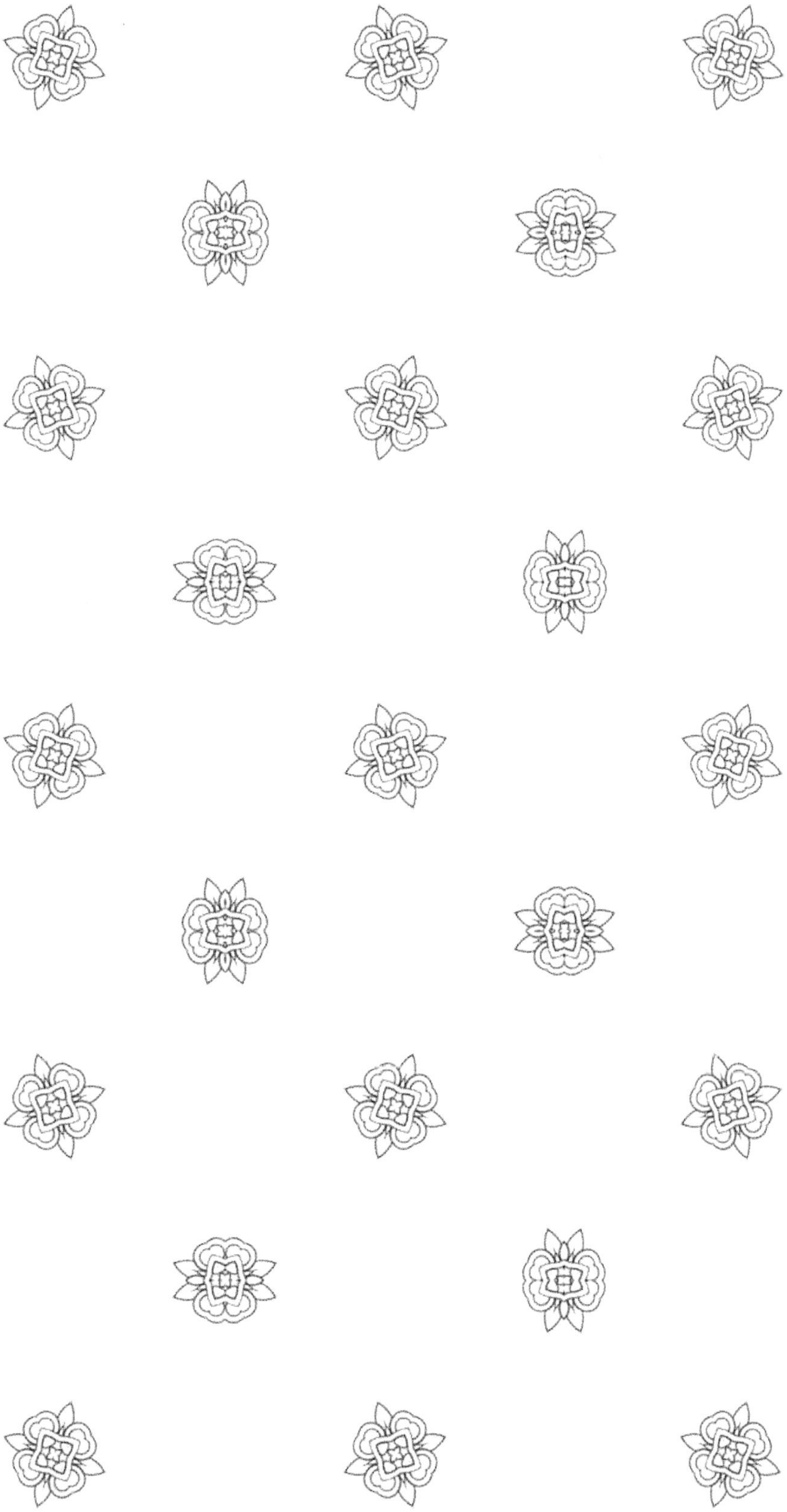

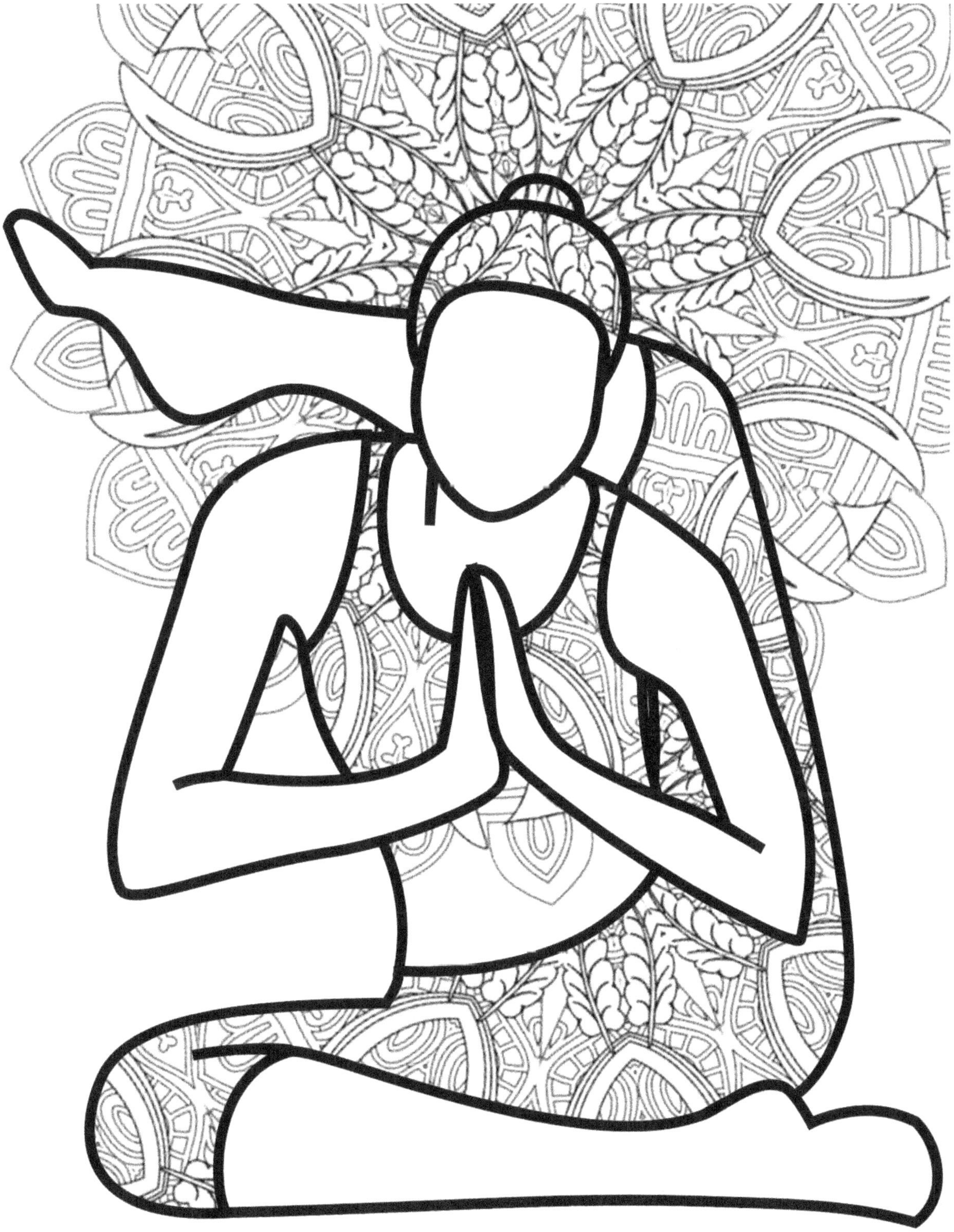

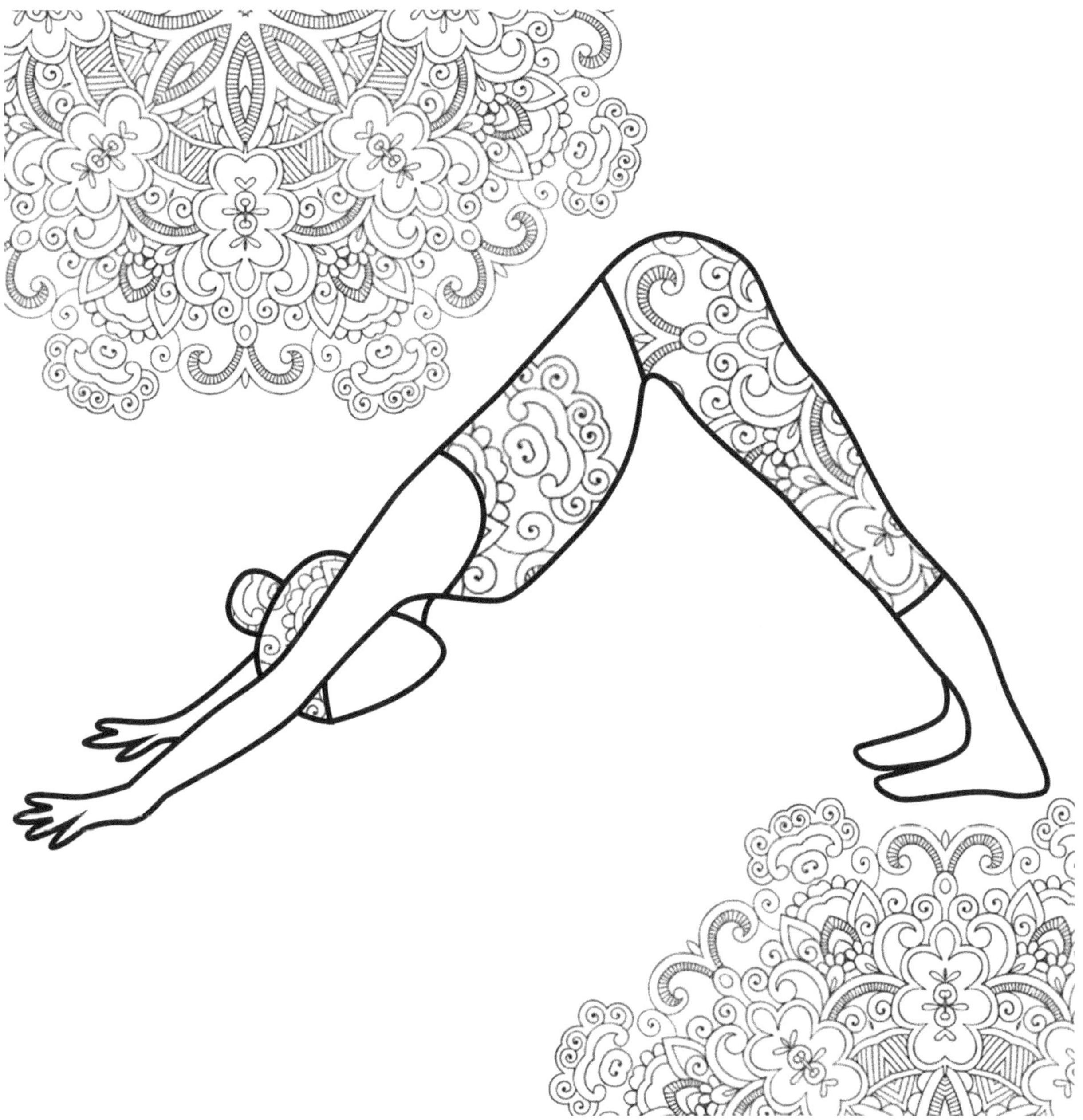

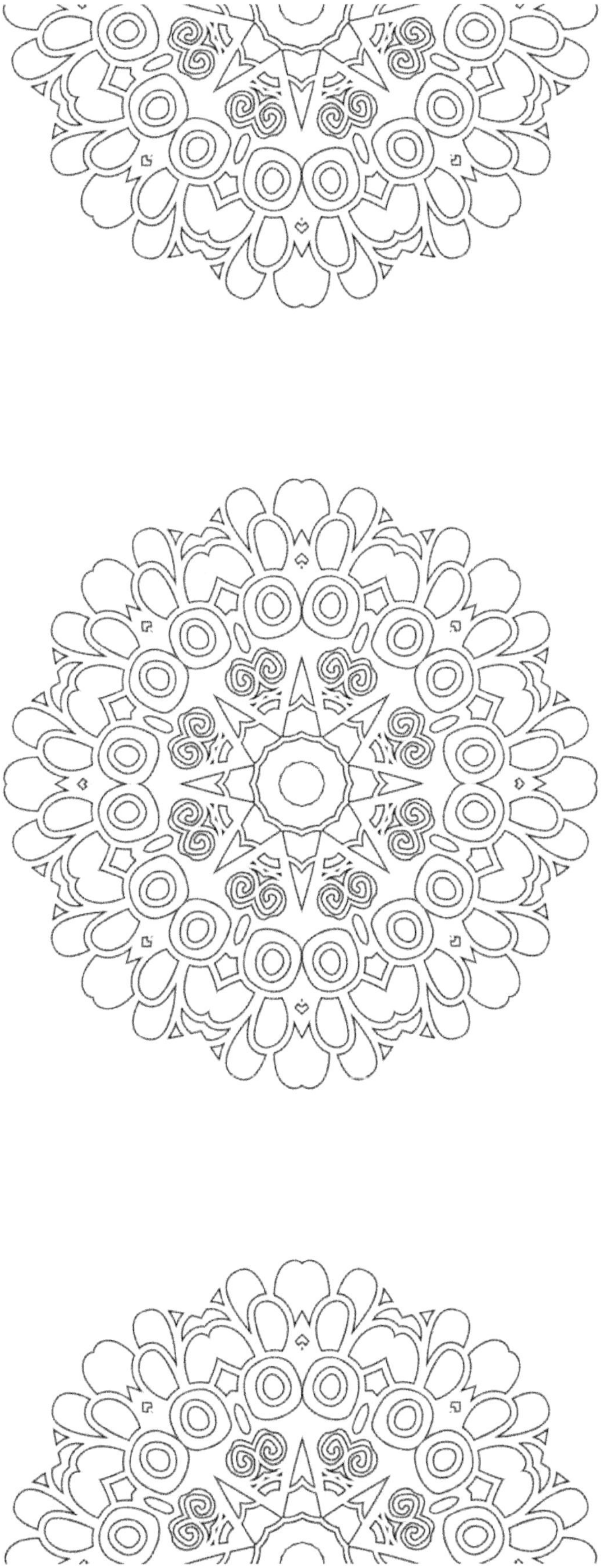

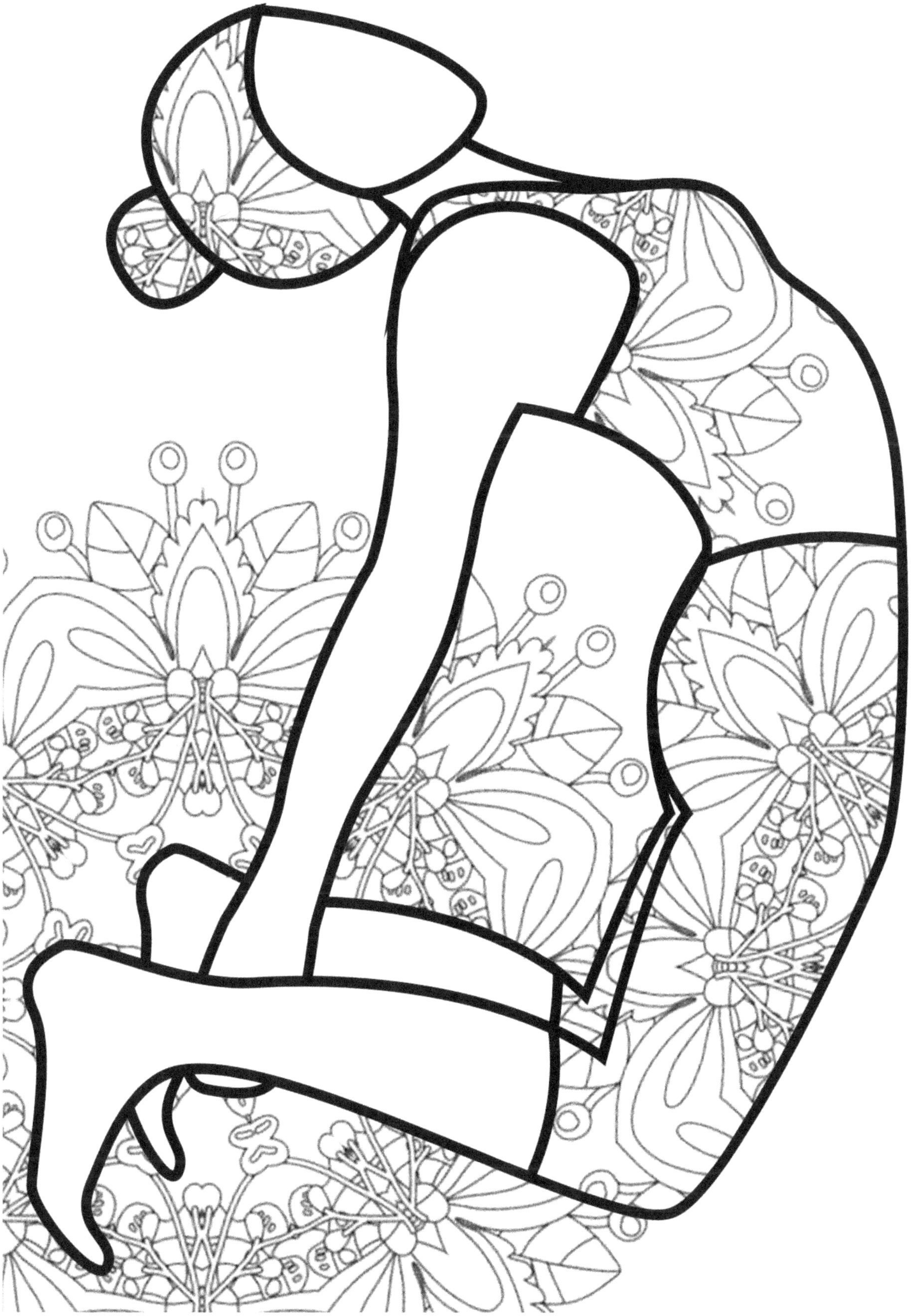

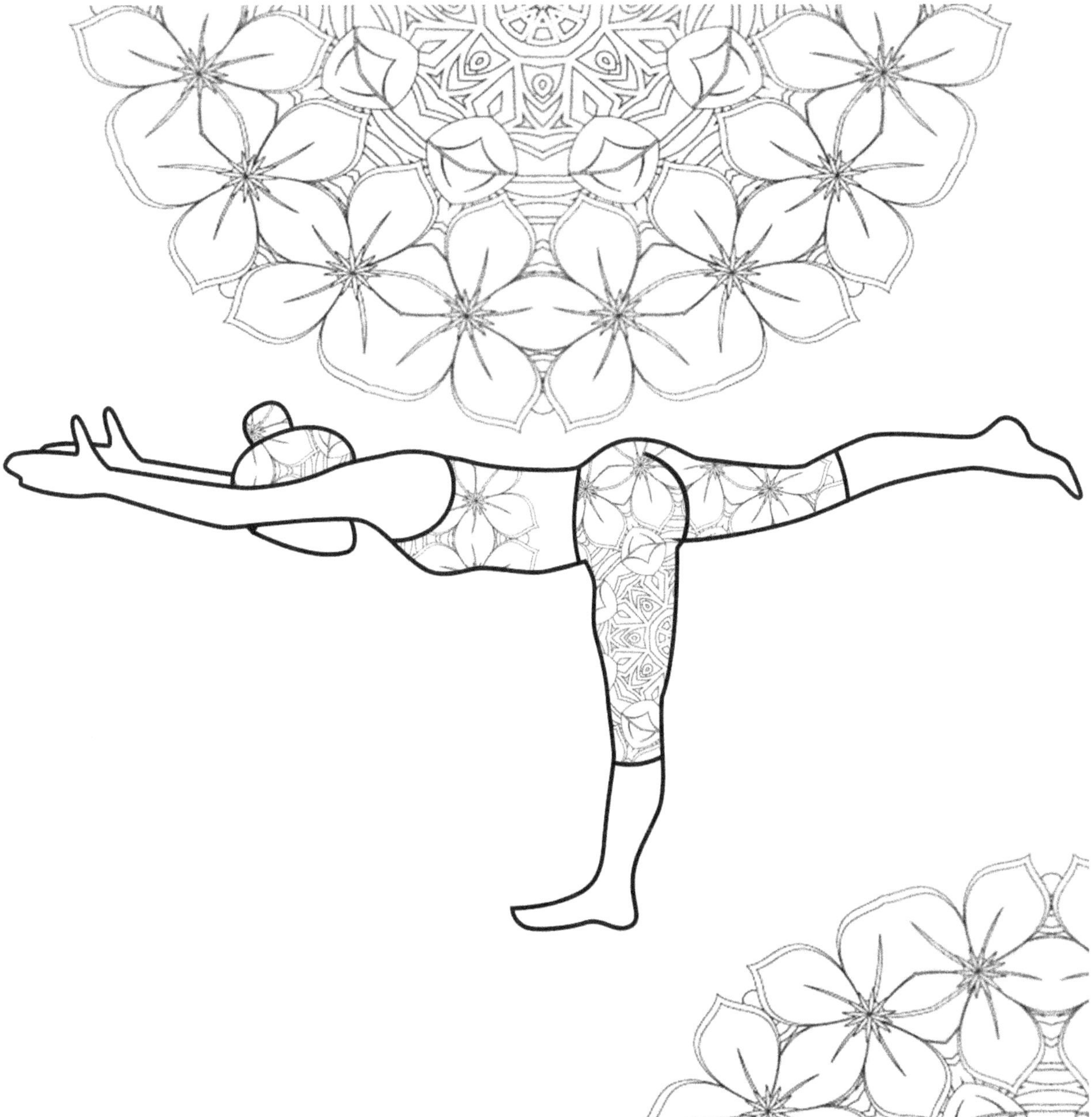

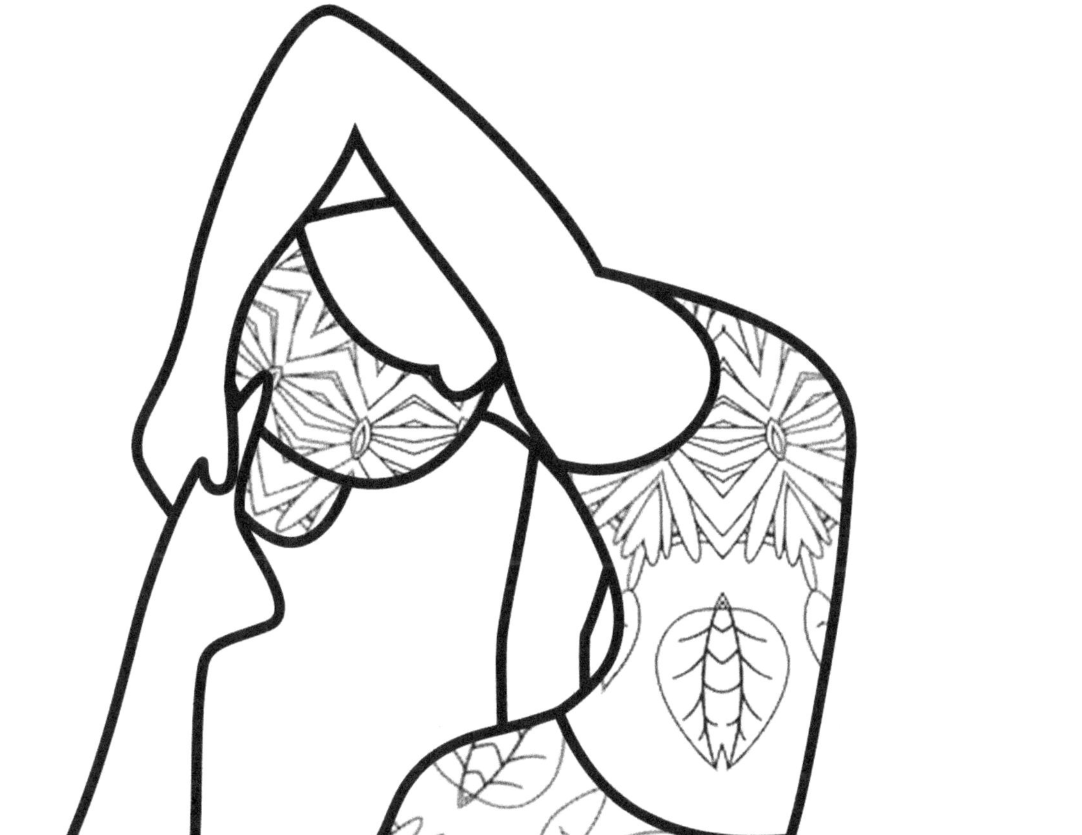

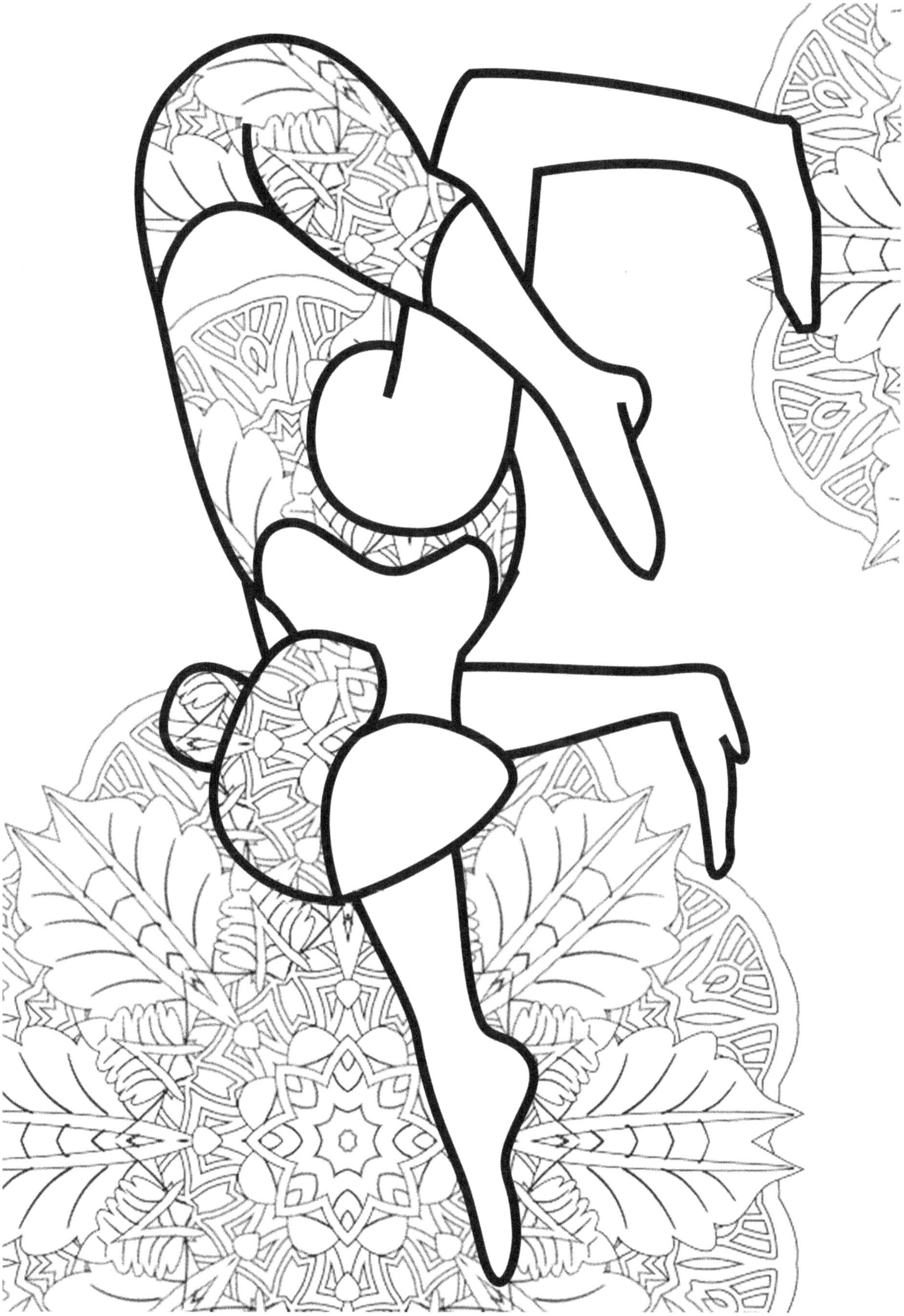

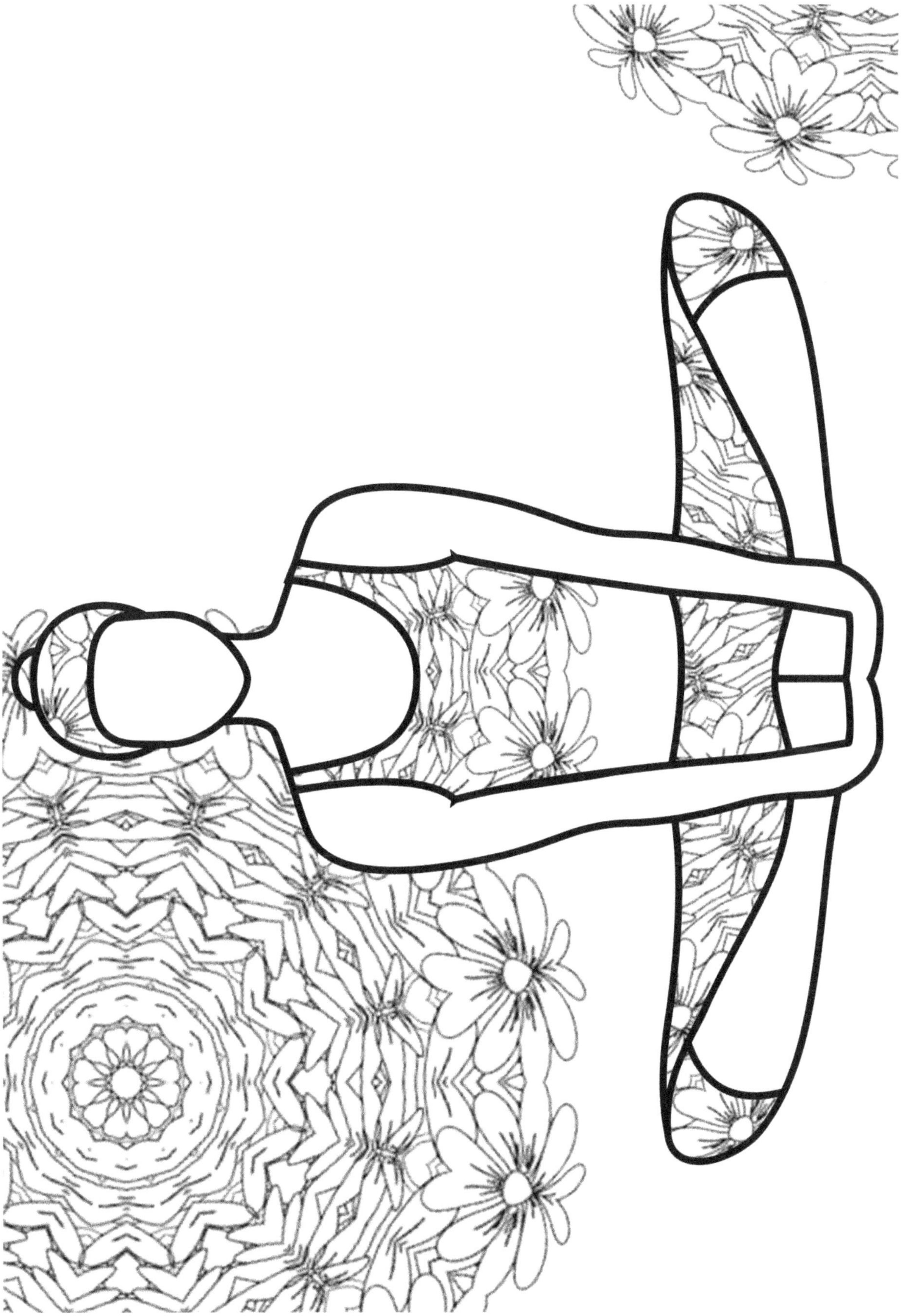

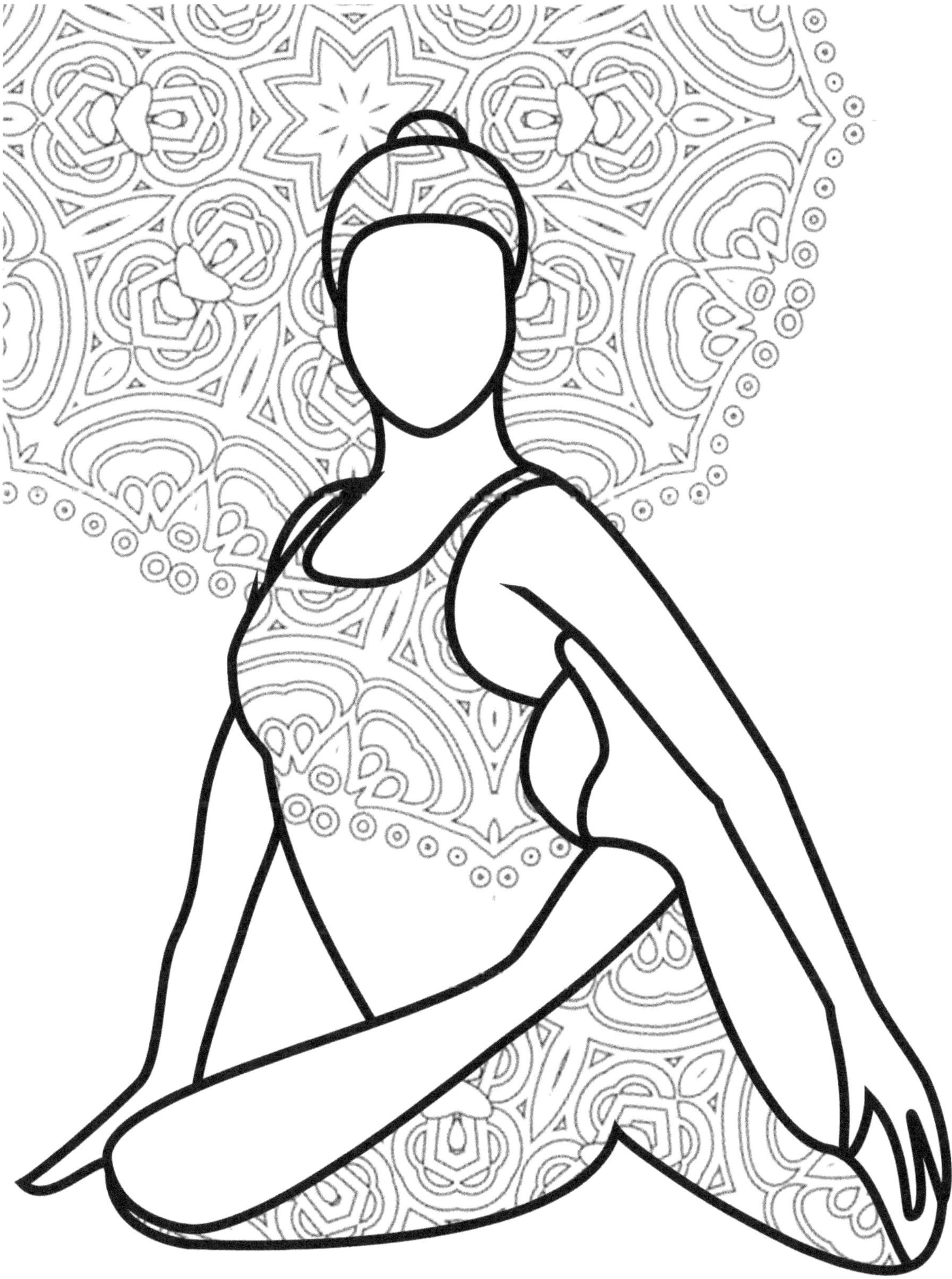

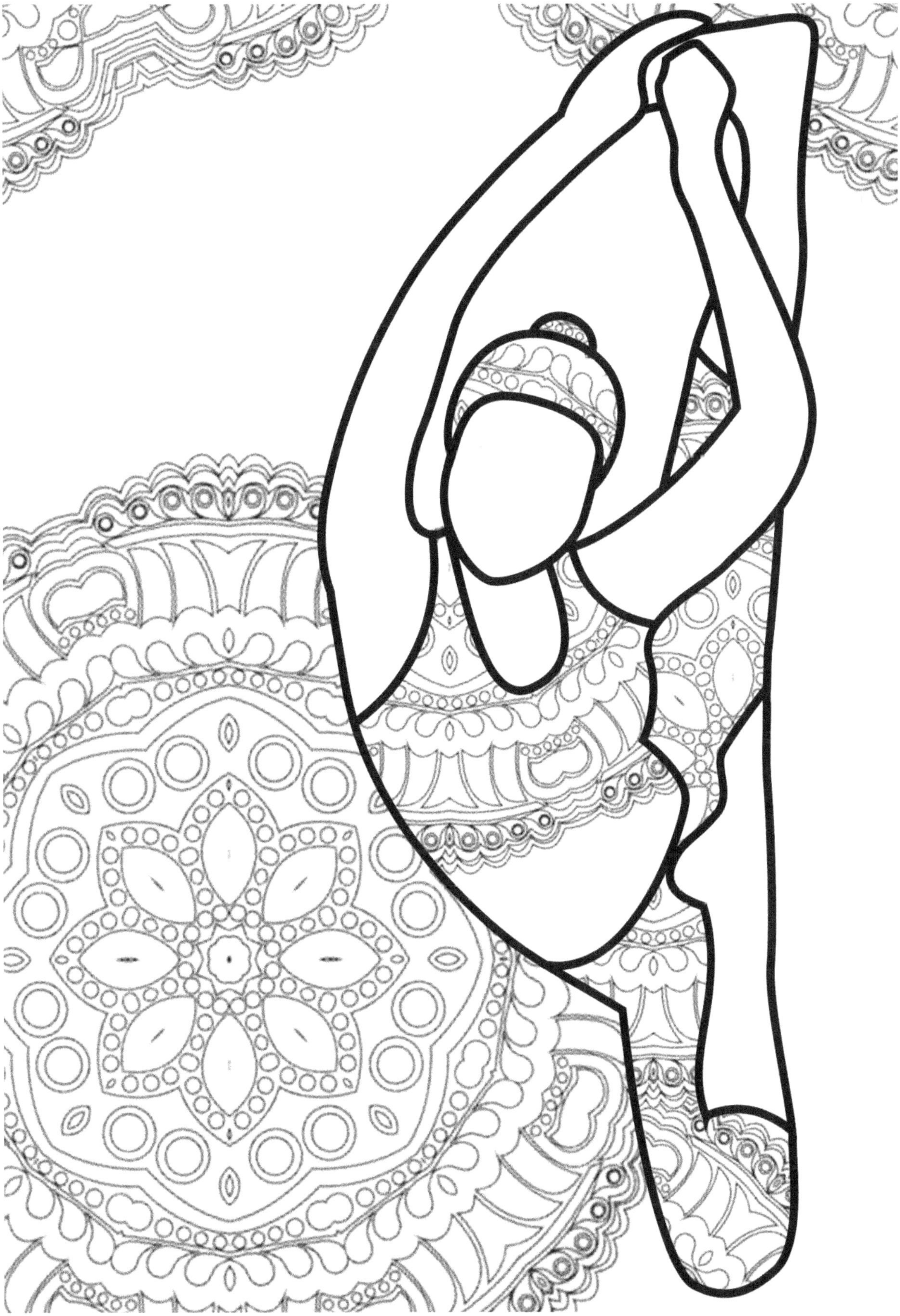

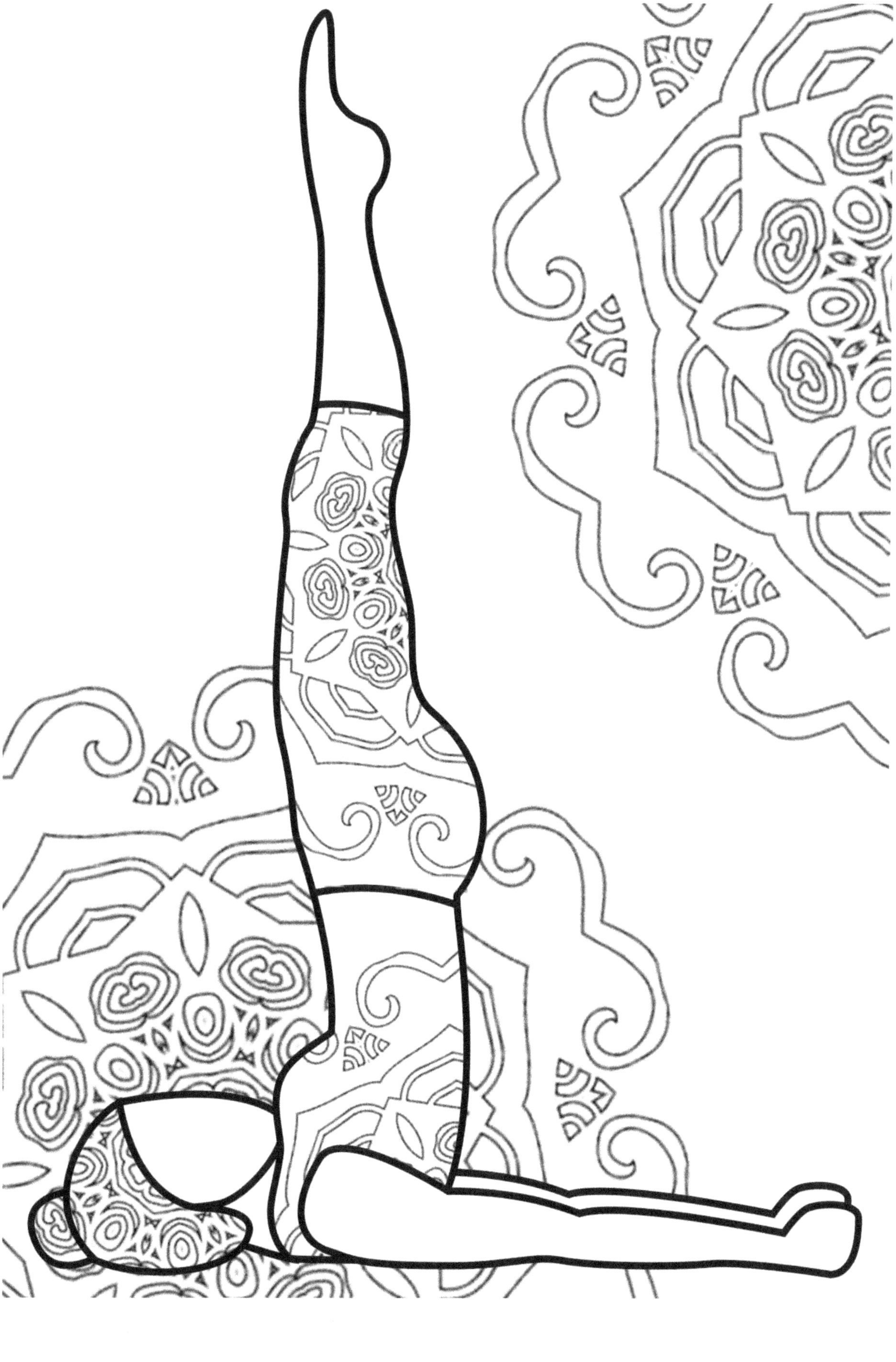

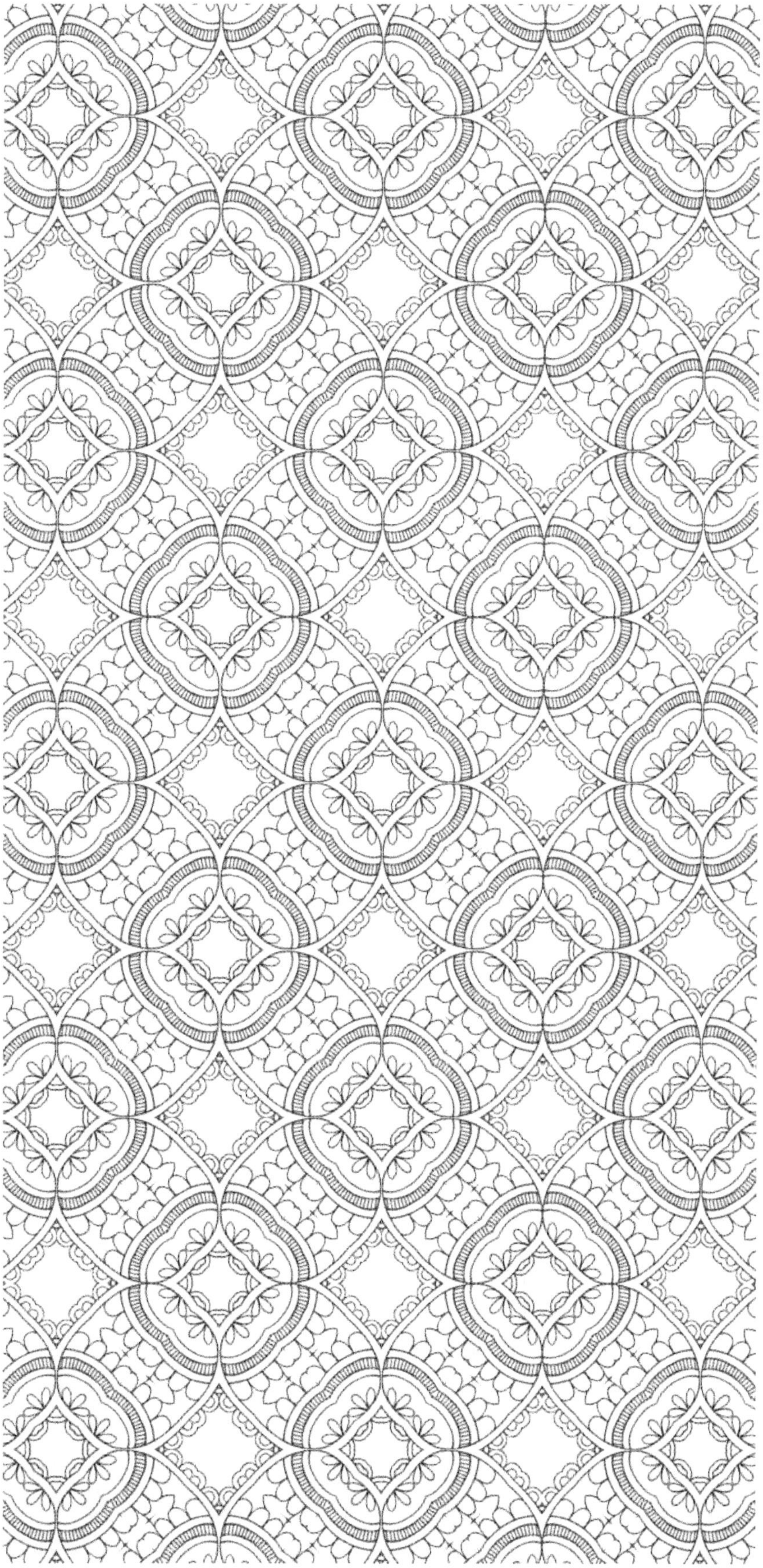

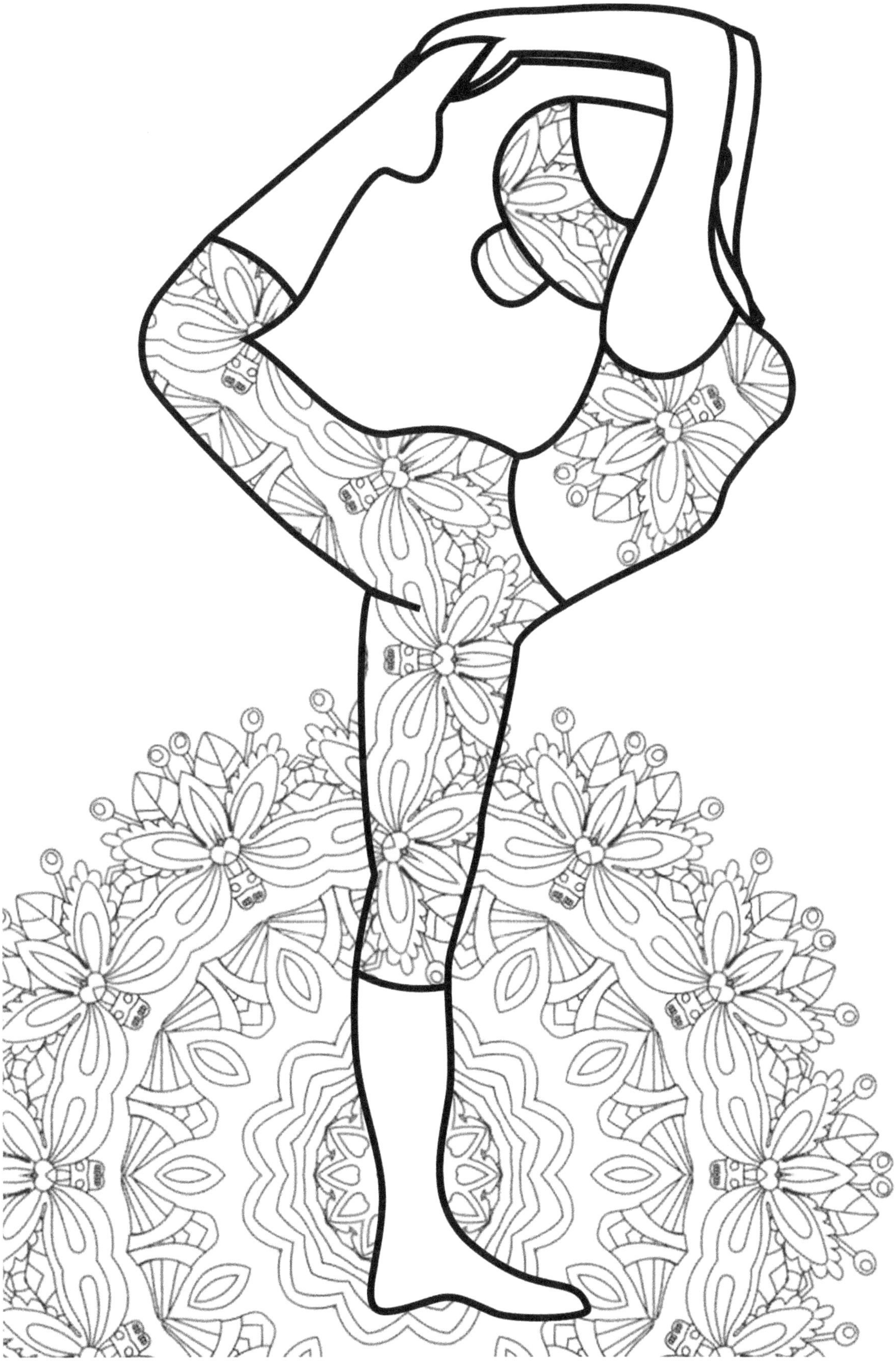

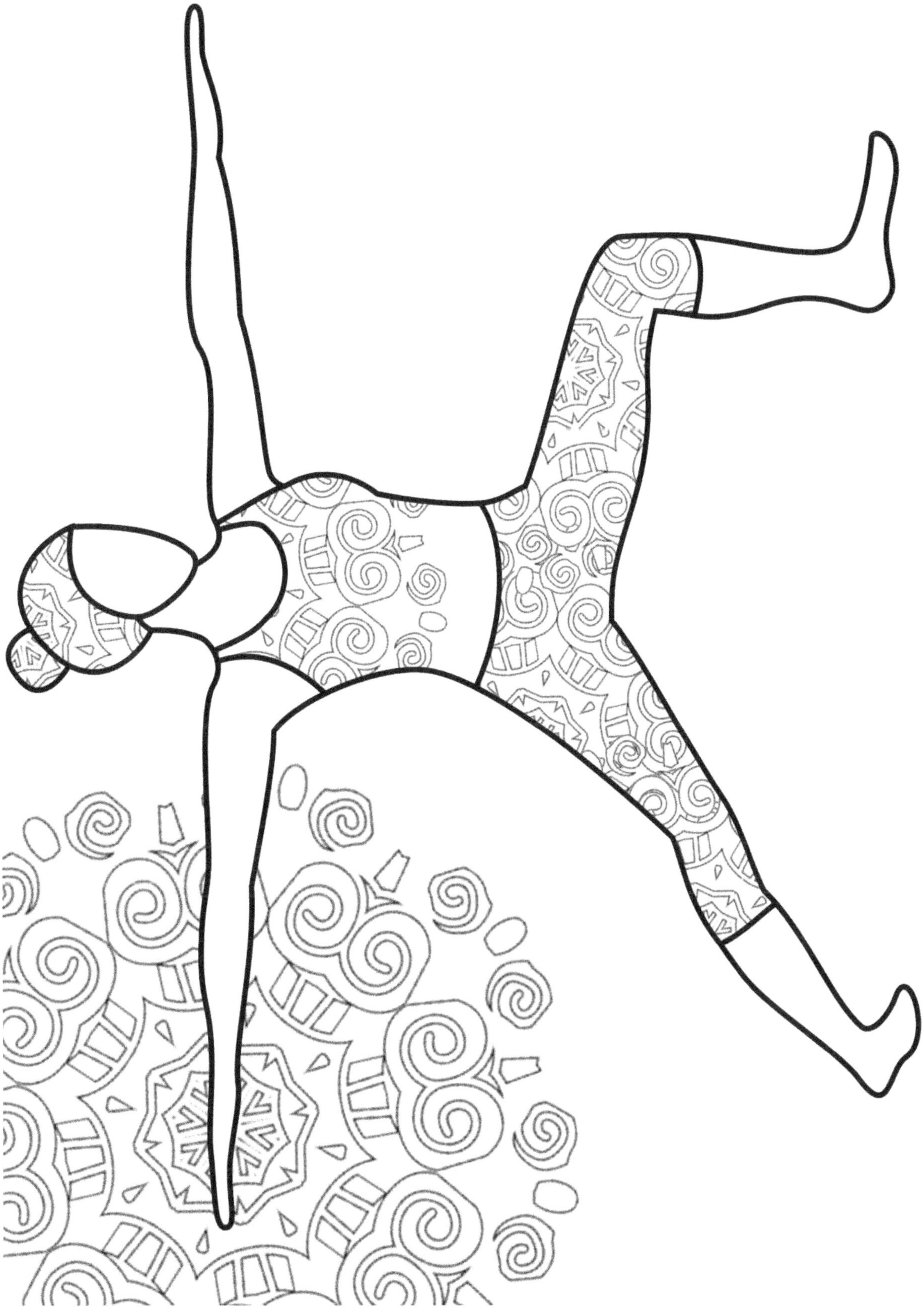

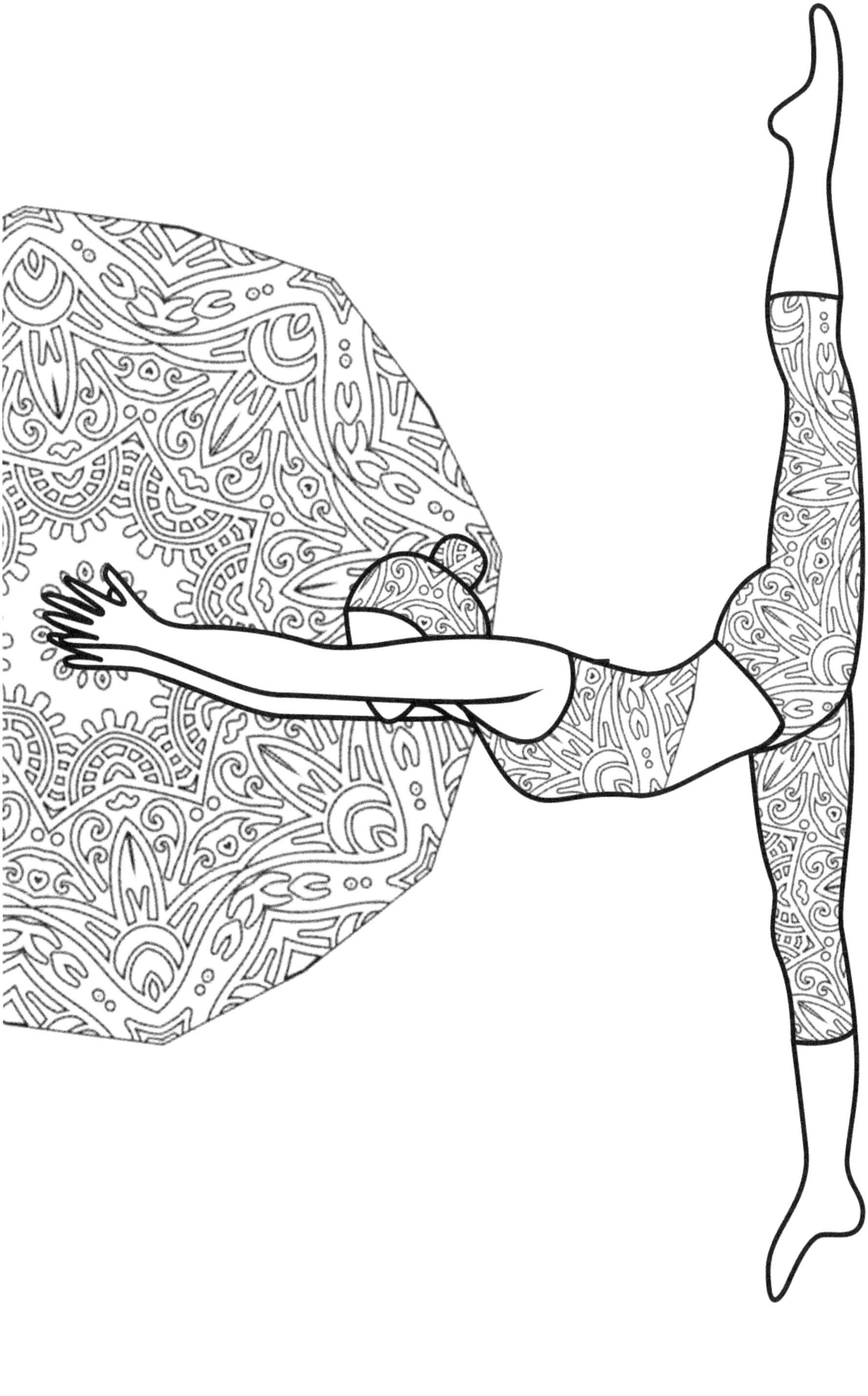

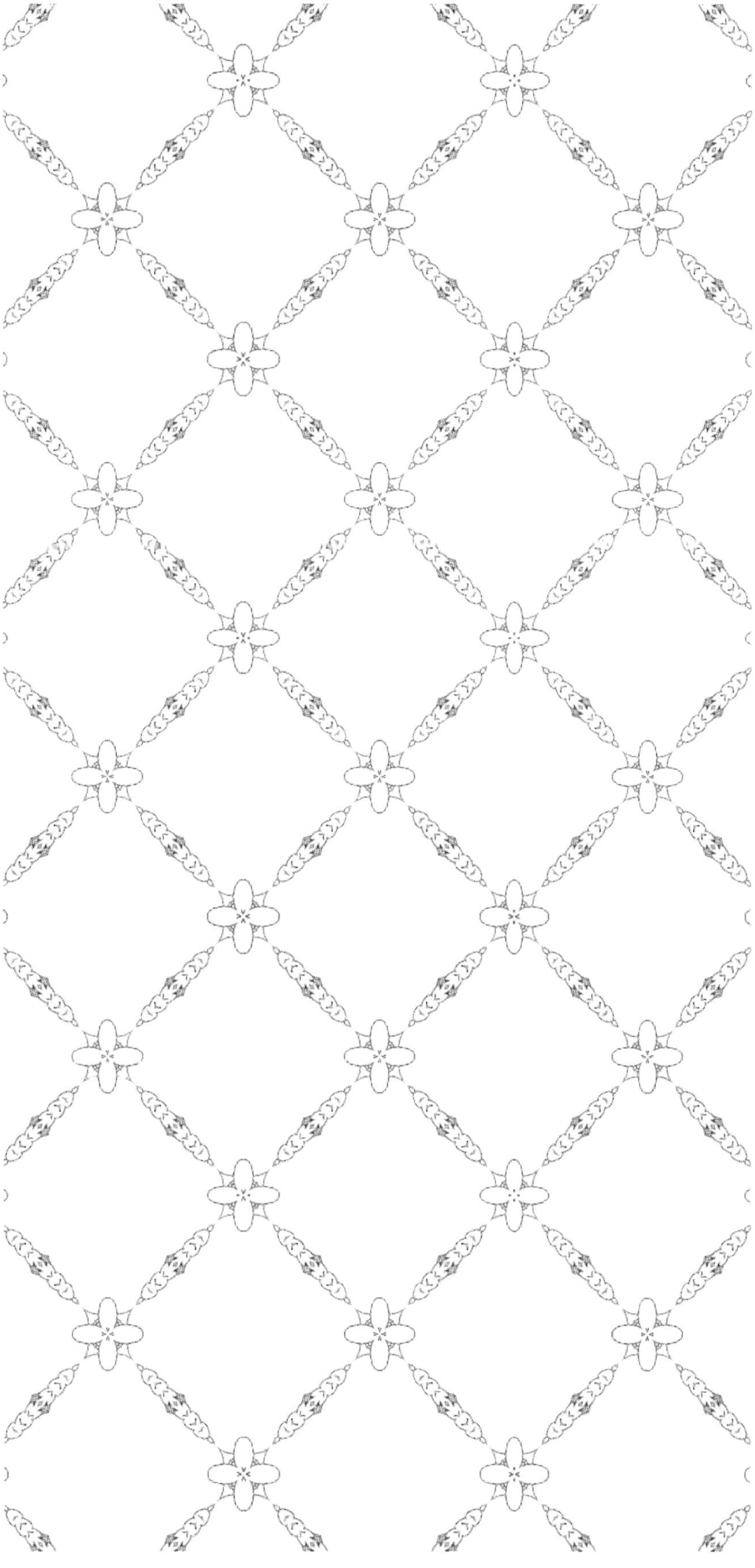

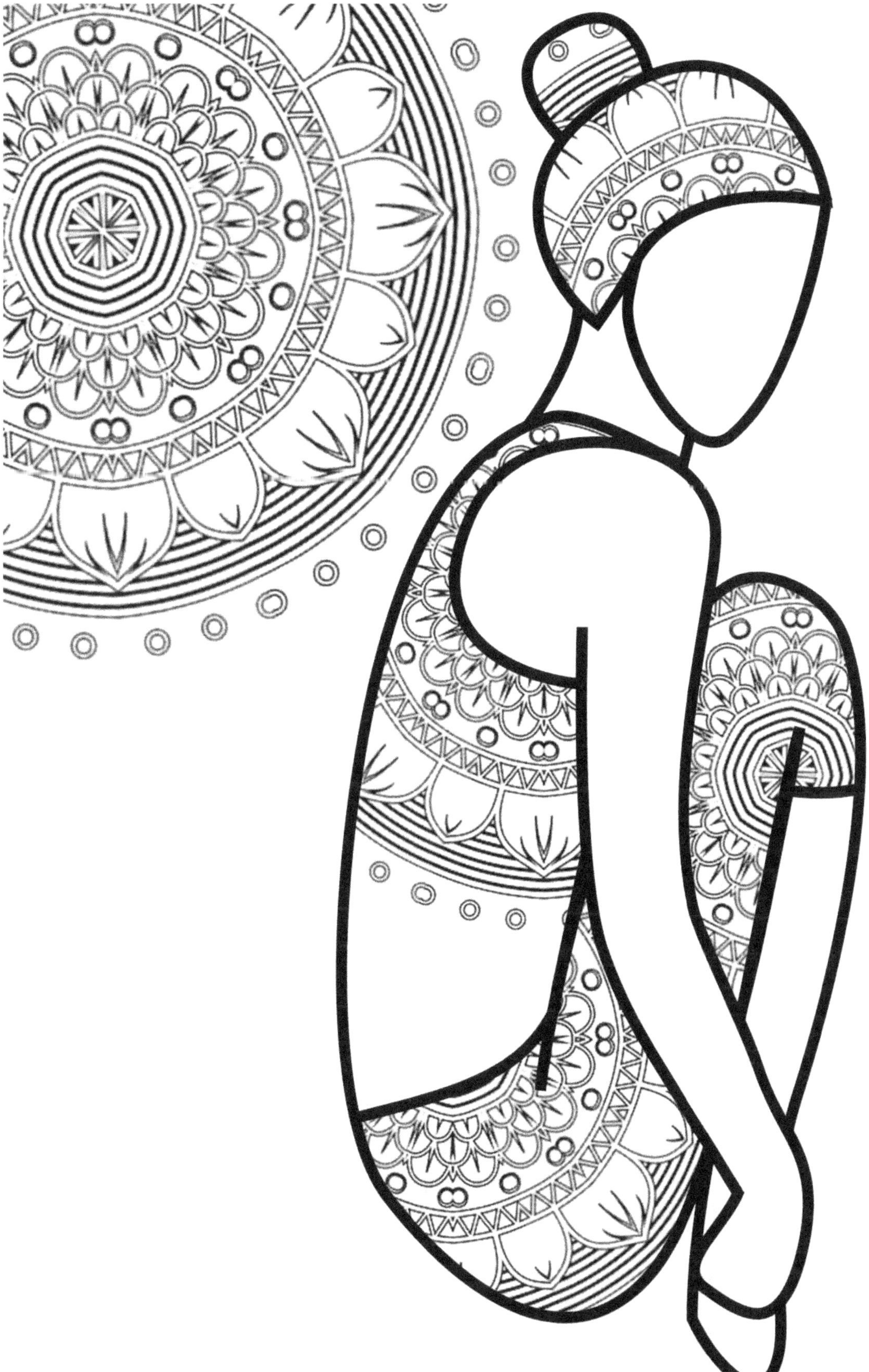

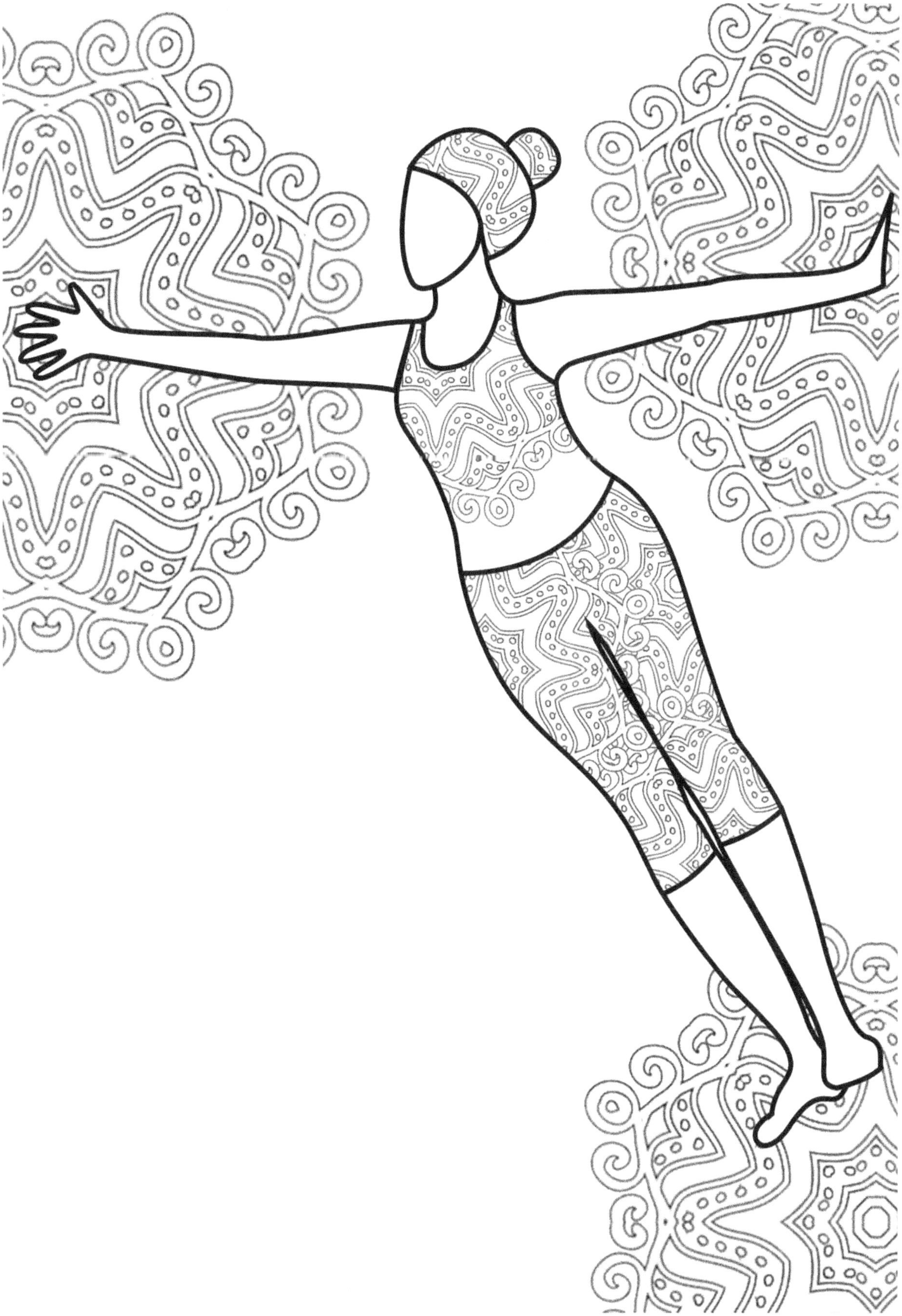

www.ingramcontent.com/pod-product-compliance
Lightning Source LLC
Chambersburg PA
CBHW081858280526
45789CB00007B/2754
9781537409542